Praise for

HONORING SERGEANT CARTER

"Extraordinary. Packed with jewels of America's racial and cultural history too often hidden from view."

—*Booklist*

"A well-grounded exposé."

—*Kirkus Reviews*

"An important and inspiring story of a young woman's unceasing effort to restore full glory to the memory of a true American hero. Both fascinating and disturbing in turn, it details one man's courage and commitment to country, his deep and abiding love for his wife, and the unraveling of their life together in the face of racial prejudice and post–World War II paranoia. It should be required reading for all Americans who value truth."

—Robert Kerrey, president of
the New School University,
former Nebraska senator and governor,
and author of *When I Was a Young Man*

"The extraordinary story of Medal of Honor winner Sergeant Eddie Carter is one that every American

should know—so that no hero will ever again suffer similar racial or political injustice from their government."

"*Honoring Sergeant Carter* celebrates heroism and condemns
injustice. The authors begin with an act of courage and
investigate why the Army forced from its ranks the heroic
soldier who performed this deed and withheld for more
than fifty years the Medal of Honor he deserved."

ALLENE G. CARTER was born and raised in Chicago. Through her father, Jesse Vaughn, a widely respected union organizer in the Chicago stockyards, Allene was at an early age introduced to the importance of the labor and civil rights movements in the African-American community. In 1973, she married Edward Carter III, the son of Sergeant Carter. When Sergeant Carter was posthumously awarded the Medal of Honor in 1997, Allene began a determined and ultimately successful quest to clear his name of unjust charges that had been used to ban him from the Army in 1949.

ROBERT L. ALLEN teaches African American and Ethnic Studies at the University of California at Berkeley and is an editor of *The Black Scholar* journal. His previous books include *Brotherman: The Odyssey of Black Men in America* (edited with Herb Boyd) and *The Port Chicago Mutiny: The Story of the Largest Mass Mutiny Trial in U.S. Naval History.*

HONORING
SERGEANT
CARTER

A Family's Journey to Uncover
the Truth About an American Hero

ALLENE G. CARTER
AND ROBERT L. ALLEN

AMISTAD
An Imprint of HarperCollinsPublishers

HarperCollins books may be purchased for educational, business, or sales promotional use. For information, please write: Special Markets Department, HarperCollins Publishers Inc., 10 East 53rd Street, New York, NY 10022.

All photographs courtesy of the Carter family archive, unless otherwise noted.

FIRST AMISTAD PAPERBACK EDITION 2004

Book design by Fearn Cutler de Vicq

Printed on acid-free paper

The Library of Congress has catalogued the hardcover edition as follows:
Carter, Allen, G.
Honoring Sergeant Carter : redeeming a Black World War II hero's legacy / by Allene G. Carter and Robert L. Allen.—1st ed.
p. cm.
Includes bibliographical references.
ISBN 0-06-621236-7
1. Carter, Edward A., d. 1963. 2. Medal of Honor—Biography. 3. African American soldiers—Biography. 4. World War, 1939–1945—Campaigns—Germany. 5. World War, 1939–1945—African Americans. 6. World War, 1939–1945—Medals—United States. 7. Carter, Allene G.
I. Allen, Robert L. 1942– . II. Title.
D796.5.U6 C36 2003
940.54'8173—dc21 2002027926

ISBN 0-06-093673-8 (pbk.)

04 05 06 07 08 ❖/RRD 10 9 8 7 6 5 4 3 2 1

In memory of my father, Jesse Vaughn (1908–1994),
the soul force in my life even when I didn't know it.
A.G.C.

For my grandson, Xye Allen Arellano, and his generation.
R.L.A.

ACKNOWLEDGMENTS

We are indebted to many individuals for generous help in bringing this project to completion. First, we are deeply grateful to all those who provided us with important assistance regarding the events recounted in these pages: Edward "Buddha" Carter, William "Redd" Carter, Fred Scott, Russell Blair, Floyd Vanderhoef, Woodfred Jordan, Andrew Nix, John Pulliams, Robert Hale, Evanda Kiel, Robert Cabbell, Neale Henderson, Walter Gaines, Octurus Culp, Earl Gipson, Jack Hill, James Harris Jr., Tamlin Harris, Nicholas Cunningham, Herbert Levy, Elsa Schulz, Wendel and Carmen Rottler, Betty Rosentrater, Daniel Chamberlain, and Peter Gravett. We also thank Marcy McGaugh for her careful transcription of interviews.

Our search for documents was greatly facilitated by Kenneth Schlessinger, archivist at the National Archives, Victor Berch and Peter Carroll at the Abraham Lincoln Brigade Archives, and Wayne Keller at the Wesleyan Archives. We also thank Joe Wilson Jr., Professor Daniel

Gibran, and Professor Ling-chi Wang for steering us to helpful research materials.

Special thanks to journalists Joseph Galloway and Del Walters, who helped bring the story to public attention.

Without the vision of publishing professionals who championed this book, it would not have seen the light of day. We are grateful to Charles Harris and Manie Barron; our agents, Richard Abate and Marie Brown; and our editor, Dawn Davis.

Finally, we thank our families, especially our spouses, Edward Carter III, and Janet Carter, for their continuing encouragement and steadfast moral support.

CONTENTS

HONORING SERGEANT CARTER

A Black Warrior in Nazi Germany

In the harsh winter of 1944–1945, the long and bitter struggle against Nazi Germany reached a decisive stage. Following early successes in the wake of D day landings in France, in mid-December the Allies were slammed with a massive counteroffensive by German forces. The German assault in the Ardennes—which would come to be known as the Battle of the Bulge—pitted a total of 600,000 Germans against 500,000 American troops. The Americans were stunned and momentarily pushed back, but heavy American bombing weakened the German forces and disrupted their supply lines, enabling the Allies to repulse the Germans and regain the initiative. The battle took a huge toll in U.S. casualties—80,000 killed, wounded, or captured—before the Allies could turn the tide. As American bombers continued to hammer German military and industrial targets, Allied forces launched a massive drive on the Rhineland. By early March, they were preparing to push into the heart of the Third Reich. To accomplish this they had to cross the

Rhine River, the major natural barrier protecting Hitler and his weakened but still dangerous armies. It was a time of fierce battles at Forbach, Freimheim, and other German towns as Allied armies raced to the Rhine. For the first time black soldiers were playing a major combat role in the Allied campaign. Staff Sergeant Edward A. Carter Jr., my father-in-law, was one of the soldiers in the forefront of this fateful assault.

Black American soldiers had not been welcomed into combat. For most of the war they were restricted to racially segregated units, working in service and support roles, such as truck drivers, stevedores, and engineers. But as a result of heavy casualties inflicted in the Battle of the Bulge, Supreme Allied Commander Dwight D. Eisenhower was compelled to find replacements wherever he could, and that included allowing black soldiers to volunteer for combat duty. This was the opportunity many black soldiers had hoped for. Thousands volunteered, and, after hasty combat training, more than 2,000 black soldiers were organized into black combat companies under white officers and attached to larger white units as part of the Rhineland campaign. These fresh reinforcements were critical to the campaign's ultimate success. But to ensure that no black soldier might command whites, black sergeants were required to relinquish their stripes.

Sergeant Carter had enlisted in the Army from his home in Los Angeles in September 1941 and had risen to the rank of staff sergeant in an all-black truck company.

Eager to get into the fight, he volunteered daily for combat duty, finally being accepted after the Battle of the
Bulge, but at the cost of his sergeant's stripes. On the
bright morning of March 23, 1945, Sergeant Carter and
his black rifle squad were riding on a tank as members of
the Fifty-sixth Armored Infantry Battalion with the
Twelfth Armored Division in General George S. Patton's
Third Army. They were advancing on Speyer, a town of
50,000 inhabitants on the Rhine. The night before, Patton's Fifth Infantry had ferried themselves in small boats
across the Rhine near Oppenheim, allowing Patton to
boast that he had beat British Field Marshal Bernard
Montgomery in the race to be the first to cross the Rhine.
Now the objective was to capture the bridge over the river
at Speyer.

Speyer was the site of an eleventh-century cathedral
where German emperors had been buried for three hundred years. It was also the champagne capital of the
Rhine Valley. A row of warehouses and breweries lined
the right side of the road as the armored column
advanced toward the town. Suddenly, the column was hit
by 88mm artillery fire coming from one of the warehouses. Jumping down from the tanks the riflemen quickly
deployed to the sides while the tanks dispersed. The officers quickly discussed what to do. Some 150 yards of open
field lay between their position and the warehouse from
which the shots were fired. Something had to be done to
silence the enemy gunners. Armed with a Thompson sub-

machine gun and a clutch of hand grenades, twenty-eight-year-old Sergeant Carter stepped forward and offered to lead the way with his squad. Of medium height and lean, compact build, Eddie Carter was a handsome man with curly black hair, reddish-brown skin, and high cheekbones. His face was relatively thin, and its dominant feature, a square jaw, was often adorned with a thin mustache. He moved, some said, with the graceful agility of a panther. While the officers set up an observation post, Carter and his three men began to advance across the open field, not realizing that the tanks were not following.

"Jerry opened up with everything he had," Carter later recalled. "Our small group was cut to pieces." One man was killed almost immediately by intense small-arms fire. Carter ordered the other two back to a protected position from which they could cover him as he advanced alone. But one of these men was killed before reaching cover, and the other was wounded. Exposed and without protective fire, Carter dashed ahead, dodging enemy bullets. Before he could hit the dirt three bullets from a German "burp" gun pierced his left arm, knocking him down. Lying on the ground looking at his bloody arm and realizing that his squad had been destroyed by the Germans, Carter became boiling mad. "The hell that was being loosed by all those Germans convinced me that I only had a few minutes to live," he said. "I decided that if I was going to die I'd make sure some Jerries would be sent to hell."

Scrambling to his feet with his tommy gun and his string of grenades, Carter charged the machine gun that had wounded him. Tossing a grenade into the German position he permanently silenced the gun. Running hard, he lobbed two more grenades, wiping out a German mortar crew that had been shelling the American lines. Still on his feet, Carter was hit by two more bullets and knocked into the air. Bullets cut into the dirt around him as he hit the ground and crawled behind a low embankment. As he tried to see where the fire was coming from, another bullet tore into his shoulder.

Seriously wounded and in pain, Carter lay still in his sheltered position. He knew he needed to take some of the pain pills he carried. As he raised his canteen to wash down the tablets with some water, another bullet tore through his hand. "This really made me mad," he recalled, "but there wasn't much I could do."

"As I lay there I saw an entire squad of Germans coming toward me in a skirmish line. I opened fire on them with the tommy gun. Got every one of 'em."

Exhausted by his ordeal, Carter remained still. Time passed. His company officers, watching from their observation post, couldn't tell whether he was alive or dead.

Sergeant Carter began to think he should try to move to another position. Before he could do so he spotted another group of German soldiers advancing on him. He wasn't sure how many there were. But his officers, who were watching from the American lines, saw eight

Germans emerge from the warehouse and move toward Carter's position. Suddenly Carter popped up and opened fire with his submachine gun. Using three clips of ammunition he brought down all but two of the Germans, who threw up their hands and surrendered.

Now Sergeant Carter had a problem: What should he do with his prisoners? One was an officer, and the other an enlisted man. Carter, who could speak some German, realized that his prisoners might be able to provide useful information on German positions. In the meantime, they could help him escape. Keeping his prisoners as close to him as possible, Carter used them as shields as he struggled to make his way back to the American lines. The tactic seemed to work for a while, but then German artillery opened up on his position. Carter took cover with his prisoners behind a gutted building, but an 88mm shell exploded nearby, sending shrapnel into his legs. Fortunately, the dust thrown up by the shell-burst offered a temporary screen, obscuring his movements as he hobbled toward the American lines partly leaning on his prisoners. Three German infantrymen made a last-ditch effort to stop him, but he took them out with his trusted tommy gun.

At last, Sergeant Carter reached the protection of the American lines and handed his prisoners over to the astonished officers. The officers were concerned about his wounds and wanted to rush him to a field hospital, but Carter insisted on first giving them information he had gathered about German gun positions. Under interrogation the prisoners also gave valuable information about German positions that greatly helped the advance into Speyer.

The retreating Germans managed to destroy the bridge, but that did not stop the American assault. Engineers built a treadway bridge that allowed the U.S. forces to cross the Rhine. Virtually single-handedly, Sergeant Carter's heroic actions had defeated a determined German effort to halt the Twelfth Armored's advance in the Rhineland campaign.

Sergeant Carter was eventually evacuated to an Army hospital to recover from his wounds. Within a month he slipped out of the hospital and made his way back to his company, where he remained as a combat soldier through the final weeks of the war, then returned home to his family in Los Angeles. Sergeant Carter was awarded the Purple Heart for his injuries, and for his heroism against the German troops he received the Distinguished Service Cross, the nation's second-highest award for valor in war. That he deserved the Medal of Honor, the nation's highest award for valor, eventually would be recognized, but not until long after his death.

CHAPTER ONE

REDISCOVERING A HERO

That my husband's father was a war hero who played a pivotal role in the Rhineland campaign during World War II was never fully known to us until we got a call on May 2, 1996, a call that would change our lives. The caller, Gloria Long, asked to speak to Mildred Carter, Sergeant Carter's widow. For several years Mildred had lived with her son, my husband, and our family. She suffered from Alzheimer's disease. I explained to the caller that Mildred was not well, that I was her daughter-in-law, and that perhaps I could help her. Ms. Long said that she was a public relations liaison person with the Department of Veterans Affairs. She was calling to tell us that the White House was planning to award the Medal of Honor, the nation's highest award for valor in combat, to several African-American soldiers who served in World War II. One of the recipients was to be Sergeant Edward A. Carter Jr.

I was flabbergasted, and somewhat disbelieving. My mind was racing. I knew that my father-in-law, who died in 1963, was a soldier in the war. I had heard a little about his wartime service from my husband, Edward (whom we all knew as "Buddha," a nickname given to him by his father because he was so chubby as a baby), and other family members, but this award was completely unexpected. Ms. Long said that plans were being made to present the awards at a ceremony at the White House, although the date hadn't yet been set. Unfortunately, in 1973, a fire had destroyed the building in St. Louis that housed certain military records, including Sergeant Carter's. Could the family help in reconstructing his tour of duty in the Army? The White House was going to prepare press releases, there would be articles in the press, and they needed information and pictures. I was stunned. Yes, I managed to say, we would help.

Mildred couldn't follow the details, but she understood enough to know that Eddie was going to be honored. "Finally. He deserves it," she kept saying. "He deserves it. He deserves it." William, Buddha's brother who lived in Washington state, was also excited, but his reaction was affected by a stroke from which he was recovering. Buddha, on the other hand, had always been withdrawn with regard to his father. Initially, I didn't get a big response from him.

I later learned through Gloria Long that, in 1992, the Army had decided to commission a study to determine why no black soldiers were given the Medal of Honor during World War II. Black soldiers had won the medal in every other major American conflict, including the Civil War. Some 1.2 million black Americans served in the U.S. military during World War II, more than in any other war. A number of soldiers, including my father-in-law, won the Distinguished Service Cross, the second-highest award, but of the 294 Medals of Honor awarded, not one went to a black soldier. Some black veterans speculated that this was no accident. Pressured by the black press, civil rights groups, and veterans and their families, and facing the possibility of congressional action, the Army decided to look into the matter.

The study was undertaken by a team of scholars, including Daniel K. Gibran, then a professor at Shaw University in Raleigh, North Carolina. After fifteen months of investigation the team produced a 272-page report concluding that the racial climate and practice within the Army during World War II accounted for the lack of black Medal of Honor recipients. Specifically, the Army's policies of segregation and exclusion of blacks from combat limited the opportunities for black soldiers to earn the Medal of Honor. In addition, the report said, racism in the Army undermined the effectiveness of black units in combat and may have prevented black soldiers from being nominated for the highest award. The report recommended that ten black soldiers, nine of whom had received the Distinguished Service Cross, be considered for the Medal of Honor. After reading the report, Secretary of the Army Togo West and the Army's senior uniformed leadership agreed with its recommendation and initiated corrective action. It was decided that six of the Distinguished Service Cross recipients and a winner of a Silver Star, the third-highest award for valor, would be awarded the Medal of Honor. There was only one snag: Congress would need to waive the 1952 statutory time limit on granting the award to World War II veterans. Congress was expected to vote on the issue in September and the ceremony would be held sometime after that.

The spring of 1996 had been a deeply somber time for us. In March, Buddha's brother William suffered a stroke and was hospitalized, unable to speak. In the same week, Iris, Mildred's daughter by her first marriage, also had a stroke. It was a terrible double blow. Iris was on life support for a period of time, but her condition didn't improve, so we finally had to make the decision to discontinue life support. Understandably, Mildred was very upset by the death of her daughter and her son's illness. We were also worried about how William might take the news, so we made the arrangements for Iris's funeral and buried her without telling him.

Given the sense of sadness and worry in our household, it was difficult to focus on Gloria Long's request for information about Eddie. When I asked Buddha what he could tell me about his father, he was very vague. He didn't seem to remember much, other than that he knew his father had won a medal during the war. Mildred was also vague about Eddie's war experiences. Both of them seemed to feel that Eddie had been given a "bad time" by the Army, but I couldn't get details. I couldn't tell if they simply didn't remember or didn't want to say.

Any lingering doubts we had about the Army's intentions were soon dispelled. On May 6, *U.S. News & World Report* published a long article on the government's plan to belatedly award the Medal of Honor to seven black veterans of World War II. The article was written by Joe Galloway and included brief descriptions of each of the seven candidates, only one of whom, First Lieutenant Vernon J. Baker, was still living. The others were Sergeant Edward Carter Jr., First Lieutenant John R. Fox, Private First Class Willy F. James Jr., Staff Sergeant Ruben Rivers, First Lieutenant Charles L. Thomas, and Private George Watson. The article included accounts of what each man had done to deserve the medal. Although brief, the description of Sergeant Carter's bravery was more than I knew before. I felt a surge of excitement as I finished the article. The reality of it all was beginning to sink in.

Over the next month William's condition improved and he was released from the hospital. Feeling that my efforts to get information from Buddha and Mildred were getting nowhere, I proposed that we all go to Washington state to have a family discussion. William (known as "Redd" in the family) was now able to speak and was being cared for by his wife, Karen. I thought that by assembling everybody in the same room with a tape recorder I could get the background information the Veterans Affairs office needed. We made the trip in July, but it was not much help after all. Redd and Buddha had been too young to remember anything about Eddie's military service. Neither did an old family friend, Gloria Arno, who was then living in Washington. She used to work with Mildred in Los Angeles but she didn't meet the family until after Eddie was out of the military. Each of them had fragments of memories, but they argued and contradicted each other and I couldn't be sure what to believe. Mil's memory was fading; she couldn't give me much. I began to feel that Mildred had somehow shielded the boys from something. It was when we returned to Los Angeles from this fruitless journey that I remembered Mildred's trunk.

In 1992, as Mildred's health started to deteriorate, Buddha and I decided to move her into our house. She had so much stuff—furniture, clothes, personal belongings—that we had to rent two storage spaces to contain it all. I remembered that there was one trunk in particular that she always wanted to keep track of. Although her memory was fading, she frequently asked me if I had the key to her trunk. Maybe there was something in the trunk that would help me with the information needed by the White House, I thought. Of course, Mildred no longer knew where the key was and she couldn't or wouldn't say what was in the trunk. This presented a dilemma. Should

I force it open? Neither Buddha nor I wanted to violate Mildred's privacy, but we were in a quandary. Everyone agreed that Eddie deserved the Medal of Honor, and we wanted to do what we could to ensure that he got full credit for his heroism.

When I pried the trunk open it was filled with dozens and dozens of letters—mostly letters from Eddie to Mildred. They included love letters, letters about plans they were making, letters about his experiences at various military bases and in the war. It was hard to put the letters down; they told a beautiful story of the love between Eddie and Mildred. Here were things I had never heard talked about in the family. There were also many photographs of Eddie in uniform, sometimes singly, sometimes with other soldiers. The pictures showed him in various locales, most of which I couldn't identify. I found photos of Eddie and Mildred together and pictures of them with Buddha and Redd as children. There was also a collection of old newspaper clippings and articles. I was thoroughly entranced. That trunk was a treasure chest.

So much material was crammed in the trunk that I decided to organize it chronologically so that I could identify and follow the sequence of Eddie's own account of his military experiences. I also wanted to reconstruct the rest of his story and find out why his success seemed clouded to his family.

I found references to Eddie having been raised by missionary parents in India and China, and having fought with both the Chinese Nationalist Army and the Spanish Loyalists. That he was recognized as a war hero when he returned from the service was quite evident: several articles published in the 1940s described his exploits in glowing terms. There were also some disturbing references. One undated article claimed that Eddie had been denied the right to reenlist, that he was barred by the Army in Fort Lewis, Washington. Apparently, the National Association for the Advancement of Colored People (NAACP) was urging the Army to allow him to reenlist. There was also a letter he wrote to Mildred in 1948 telling her not to worry about the CIC, that his record was clean and they had nothing to fear. I worried about what all this meant, especially when I learned that CIC had to do with the military Counterintelligence Corps. Was he under investigation? For what? Did it have something to do with his reenlistment problem? Whatever happened, could it reach through time and adversely affect his candidacy for the Medal of Honor?

To my relief, there was nothing in the Shaw University report to suggest that Sergeant Carter had any problems while he was in the service. Interestingly, the report mentioned a 1945 news item from the *Omaha Star*, a black newspaper, claiming that Sergeant Carter was originally recommended by his superior officers for a Medal of Honor but was denied it because of his race. According to the report, "It is possible that Carter's award recommendation began as a Medal of Honor and was then changed to a Distinguished Service Cross. Research for this study, however, has found no evidence to support such a hypothesis."

The report was going to be published as a book, under the title *The Exclusion of Black Soldiers from the Medal of Honor in World War II,* and Professor Gibran, one of the authors, called to ask if I could send him a photograph of Sergeant Carter to be used in the forthcoming book. We also talked briefly about their research in the National Archives and the Army personnel files that had been destroyed in the 1973 fire in St. Louis. It occurred to me that the National Archives might have more information on Eddie that would be useful in my research for Gloria Long and the White House, and helpful in putting my mind at ease. But a trip back east seemed a remote prospect.

In the meantime, I tried my hand at doing research closer to home. Joe Wilson, a military historian I had met, referred me to two important books: *The Hellcats,* about the Twelfth Armored Division's activities during the war, and *The Employment of Negro Troops,* by Ulysses Lee. Both books contained mentions of Sergeant Carter (although his name is incorrect in *The Hellcats*). Lee's book contained a one-paragraph description of the action at Speyer and Sergeant Carter's role in it. The context of this account was a visit on April 19, 1945, to the Twelfth Armored Division by General Benjamin O. Davis, the top-ranking black officer in the Army.

In addition to these books, William told me that Mildred once had an issue of *Ebony* magazine that contained pictures and a big story about Eddie. I wrote to the offices of *Ebony* in Chicago and was able to get a copy of the January 1947 issue, which included an article about black soldiers who won medals for bravery. The article, "Where Are the Heroes?," included two wonderful photographs of Eddie with Mildred and their young sons in Los Angeles after the war.

The tone of the article was critical. It pointedly stated that many black veterans, including those praised for heroism, returned to an America that continued to discriminate against them. It quoted Eddie as saying, "The war helped race relations by proving to America and the world that Negroes and whites could live, produce and fight a common enemy together. . . . The Negro gained much from the war but there is room for improvement, a whole lot—about 99 percent."

Congress had voted to set aside the statute of limitations on awarding the Medals of Honor to the seven soldiers. The ceremony was set for January 13, 1997. Time was pressing. In September 1996, I made arrangements to fly back east to visit the National Archives at College Park, Maryland.

Making a trip to the National Archives was not a simple thing. I had to arrange for some time off from work; I needed to make sure that Mildred's and the rest of the family's needs were taken care; and, of course, there was the expense involved. I worked as a supervisor of the 911 emergency dispatch center in Los Angeles County. With enough advance notice I could get a colleague to cover for me or arrange some vacation time. With some pre-planning and meals cooked in advance, the family could survive for a few days without me. My husband was supportive. He wasn't altogether sure why I needed to make this trip, but he knew I was doing it to help his father. We would somehow squeeze the money needed out of the budget.

That it fell to me to make the trip made sense in terms of family dynamics. When the initial call came from Gloria Long, I took it and dealt with it. I had to—Buddha and Mildred were too distraught over of William's stroke and Iris's death. The family was in crisis. If there was one thing I knew from my five years of experience as a 911 dispatcher and fourteen years as a supervisor, it was to remain calm and take things one step at a time. First, help Buddha and Mildred deal with their grief and worry. Then, gather information for the White House as best I could. Once I started the research, Buddha and Mildred, and later William, encouraged me to follow through, although with all of them there seemed to be a lingering reticence, an almost palpable uneasiness. They wanted Eddie to get the Medal of Honor, but they seemed apprehensive about where my research might lead. Mildred could no longer tell me what had happened. Buddha and Redd never really knew; they only knew the bad feelings that Eddie's military experience had left in the family. The feelings were painful and they didn't want to talk about them. Their inner conflict made it impossible for them to probe, to uncover what might be hidden in trunks or archives.

I was met at the National Archives by Kenneth Schlessinger, an archivist. I told him of the upcoming Medal of Honor event and explained that I was trying to get information for the family and for public dissemination. I wanted to see anything that might be helpful in understanding Sergeant Carter's experiences and the general situation of black soldiers in the Army during the war and any problems they might have encountered there. Mr. Schlessinger directed me to the materials used by the Shaw University researchers and other important record groups. These included several sets of records and memos from Eddie's unit, the Fifty-sixth Armored Infantry Battalion, that detailed the battalion's movements in March 1945 at the time of the attack on the German town of Speyer. Sergeant Carter was not mentioned, but the maps, handwritten notes, and memos made the whole thing more real for me. Here were firsthand documents that recorded actions where Sergeant Carter was present. I leafed through the fading papers and tried to imagine what it was like for him. I realized that I could never know what he went through, but holding notes and messages that had been written while the fighting was actually going on made me feel close to Eddie.

I also found War Department press releases that praised the bravery and fighting spirit of black troops in the all-black Ninety-second Infantry Division in Europe, the Ninety-third in the Pacific, the 761st Tank Battalion, and the 332d Army Air Force Fighter Group—the famed Tuskegee Airmen—stationed in Italy. One press release applauded the hundreds of black troops originally assigned to service units who, like Eddie, had volunteered for combat duty as riflemen.

The other documents I found with Schlessinger's help were more disturbing. For example, there was a series of reports assessing the use of Negro rifle platoons in the Army during the war. Although the reports generally concluded that the black infantry units, composed of volunteers, performed well in combat, almost all of the authors recommended against forming racially integrated fighting units. Instead they recommended continuation of the policy at that time of limited use of all-black units under white (or possibly black) officers within larger white combat units. In other words, black troops might be allowed into combat, but only in segregated units.

Evidence of discrimination against and mistreatment of black soldiers was plentiful in a file of letters and reports that had been sent to William M. Hastie, a respected black judge who was dean of the Howard University Law School. In 1940 he was appointed Civilian

Aide on Negro Affairs by Secretary of War Henry Stimson. Among other things, Hastie tracked racial incidents in the military. The material in the file was chilling. It included a report of the lynching in 1941 of a young black soldier, Felix Hall, at Fort Benning, Georgia. There was also a report of what Hastie called the "wanton slaying" of an unarmed black soldier, Albert King, by a military policeman at Fort Benning in the same year. The military policeman was acquitted; Hall's slayers were apparently not found. In June 1942, Eddie was a sergeant in a service battalion at Fort Benning. Did he know of these killings?

Schlessinger recommended that I review some additional files that proved to be equally troubling. These were military weekly intelligence reports for 1944–1946. I was surprised to see that the Army collected detailed information on the involvement of black soldiers in so-called racial situations around the country, and special attention was given to the reaction of the Negro press to these incidents. The situations commonly involved acts of racial discrimination, mistreatment, or violence against black soldiers, including incidents on military bases, or black citizens in general. The activities of the NAACP and other civil rights groups were also closely monitored. The reports were organized under headings such as "Organizations Fomenting Racial Agitation" and "Potential Racial Disturbances." Black soldiers or sailors observed speaking out against or actively resisting discrimination were described as "attempting to create racial unrest."

No part of the country seemed exempt from the pry-
ing eyes of military intelligence. Some areas, however,
were described as "sensitive." Los Angeles, where Eddie
and his family lived before and after the war, was often
high on the list of "sensitive" areas because, as a report on
January 5, 1946, stated, "of the heavy concentration of
Negro workers, unrest in the Los Angeles Harbor Area
and current government cutbacks." Other cities in California, and sometimes Washington state, were occasionally identified as sensitive for similar reasons.

Some of the weekly intelligence reports included sections on "communists and fellow travelers." Reading these
I came across a reference to the *Daily World,* the Communist Party's newspaper. I remembered that one of the
news clippings about Eddie's heroism that I found in Mildred's trunk came from the *Daily World.* Now, a few pages
further on in the intelligence report, I found a reference to
a "Welcome Home, Joe" dinner held in Los Angeles and
sponsored by an organization called American Youth for
Democracy. A parenthetical comment in the report
described this group as a "CP [Communist Party] organization." I felt a cold shiver: this dinner was mentioned in
the same *Daily World* clipping I had found in Mildred's
trunk. The intelligence report went on to quote an
unidentified Negro newspaper as writing that "embittered" World War II veterans honored at the dinner
denounced the "so-called democracy for which they
fought." These veterans said that they returned "to find

America more prejudiced than before and intolerance at an all-time new high." Having just read of the "racial situations" encountered by black soldiers and civilians, I didn't find the views expressed by the veterans at the dinner very surprising. But it was disturbing to find an event that Eddie attended alluded to in these intelligence reports. His name was not mentioned specifically, but I knew his attendance had been mentioned in the newspaper coverage.

An FBI report I examined did not relieve my worry. Entitled "Foreign Inspired Agitation Among American Negroes in the Los Angeles Field Division," the November 21, 1944, report stated that white homeowners protective associations were "becoming more active against negro encroachment" and were trying to establish restrictive covenants to prevent blacks from buying homes. Anonymous literature was being circulated, it continued, advocating the boycotting and disenfranchisement of Negroes. The U.S. Attorney in Los Angeles had advised that circulation of such literature did not constitute a violation of civil rights. However, the black press and civil rights groups had "expressed considerable concern over the circulation of such literature."

As I browsed through the seventy-eight-page report, a subhead that read "Eastside Chamber of Commerce—Negro" caught my eye. The name rang a bell. Again I remembered clippings from Mildred's trunk, articles published in May 1946 reporting some upheaval in the leader-

ship of the Eastside Chamber of Commerce in Los Angeles, resulting in Eddie being appointed director of public
relations for the organization and chairman of its veterans
committee. The FBI account seemed innocuous enough.
An informant described the organization as "vitally interested in improving health conditions among the negroes,
especially wiping out venereal disease, which, according to
military and naval authorities, was showing an alarming increase among the servicemen." Then I came to the
lines: "There are certain members of the organization
which might be considered 'striped.' By striped he [the
FBI informant] meant radicals whom some people might
consider as Communists. These members, however, kept
their activity on such a plane so as not to reflect on the
chamber or the community as a whole and were therefore
allowed to maintain their membership." Of course, Eddie
was in the war in 1944, but was the Eastside Chamber of
Commerce still under surveillance in 1946? Was Eddie suspected of Communist Party involvement?

I returned from the National Archives with more questions than when I left. I worried that perhaps Eddie did
have some connection with communists, and that this was
the source of his problems. There seemed to be a fear in
the family that Eddie's problems with the Army might
have been his own doing. Could those problems rise again
to be his undoing now? For the most part all that the gov-

ernment's extensive spying on black soldiers and the black community turned up was a determined refusal by African Americans to any longer accept segregation, discrimination, and mistreatment. The government was treating civil rights activism as criminal. Anytime black people voiced or acted out their objections to racism, both the military and the FBI saw this as subversive. Eddie was not the kind of man to meekly accept mistreatment. He was not belligerent, but he would have voiced his objections. He would have said that the country needed some serious improvement, as he did in the *Ebony* magazine article. Was this what they had against him? I didn't know. I had questions, but I hadn't found any answers.

Earlier in the spring of 1996 a scandal broke in Los Angeles about cemeteries. Remains reportedly were being dug up and other bodies buried in the graves. We heard a news report about it, and Mildred started pressing me to go to the cemetery to make sure Eddie's body hadn't been dug up. To my surprise, she described exactly where the grave was located in the cemetery, in a corner by a big tree. She said, "I know this because I used to go there after work, and I'd lay on his grave and cry. I would say 'Why did you leave me? Why did you leave me?' I did that many a night."

When I visited the place, it turned out to be an old veterans cemetery and not very well maintained. I found the gravesite where Mildred said it would be. The place was somewhat unkempt but Eddie's headstone was there and the grave appeared to be undisturbed . . . except for what looked like a plastic bag lying next to the headstone. Thinking it was trash, I picked it up. Inside I discovered a newspaper article about Eddie being nominated for the Medal of Honor. Who had put this here? There was no note or name, only the clipping. I was mystified. I tucked the clipping in my purse. I had brought a camera so I took a photo of the grave and the headstone to reassure Mildred. The headstone read: "Edward A. Carter, Jr. SFC, U.S. Army, World War II, DSC, BSM, PH & 2 OLC. May 26, 1916–January 30, 1963."

I made my way out of the cemetery, occasionally nearly tripping over gopher holes, and feeling increasingly annoyed that this neglected site was Eddie's final resting place. As the grave of a soldier about to be honored with the highest award his nation could give, it seemed sadly inappropriate. It was not a hero's burial place. For weeks I couldn't get the image of Eddie's grave out of my mind.

Then, suddenly, I had an epiphany. I knew about the National Cemetery at Arlington and that many soldiers and national leaders were buried there. Eddie didn't get the hero's burial he deserved when he died, but now maybe he could.

Once again I made a phone call to Gloria Long. She didn't know what could be done, and she passed me along to an office at Arlington National Cemetery. The officials at Arlington were not happy about my proposal. Why did I want to do this? They said they were going to come to Los Angeles and put a new headstone on his grave. If they did what I wanted for him, they would have to do it for others, they argued. They had buried him once and they weren't going to bury him again. I stayed calm. "My question to you is," I said, "does winning the Medal of Honor qualify him to be in Arlington?" A reluctant "yes" was the reply. "Then we want him moved there," I said. "We can't pay for it," they countered. "Would you allow his body to be transported on a military flight?" "No." They were not giving up anything, but they couldn't deny that Eddie was qualified to be buried at Arlington.

It was time for another family council. I talked with Mildred and Buddha and explained that this was something Eddie was qualified to have and he deserved it as a Medal of Honor winner. Mildred, especially, was thrilled. "I think it's wonderful," she said. "Let's do it." Buddha and the rest of the family agreed enthusiastically.

Money was tight, because we had had to bury Iris. But we had a sense of changing history. The family told me there had been no press coverage and no fanfare when Eddie was buried in 1963, only a small, quiet ceremony. All they had left to remember him was the flag the government provided for his casket. If we're going to do this, I said, then let's do it in a way that involves the community. I felt that people should know that a hero from our community was getting the Medal of Honor and that he was going to buried in Arlington National Cemetery.

After the *U.S. News & World Report* piece, we started getting lots of calls and correspondence from the media and people curious about Eddie. One day a letter came from a man named Joe Wilson Jr. He said his father had served in the military with Sergeant Carter in Germany, and later at Fort Lewis, Washington. Wilson's father had served in the all-black 761st Tank Battalion, a heroic unit nicknamed the "Black Panthers" that endured 183 days of continuous frontline duty in the war. The 761st had been attached to both the Third Army and the Seventh Army, and Sergeant Carter had also served in both. Joe was writing a book about the 761st Black Panther Tank Battalion. He was completing his research and wanted a picture of Eddie, whom he planned to cite in his book since Eddie was to receive the Medal of Honor. I eventually learned that he was the person who had placed the newspaper clipping at Eddie's grave. "I wanted the world to know that Sergeant Carter was getting the medal," he told me.

Joe Wilson was a godsend. Deeply interested in the history of black soldiers, Joe had played a part in the campaign that led to the Medal of Honor awards. In the months after we met he gave me several pointers about how the military functions, as well as pertinent military history, including information on the Twelfth Armored Division. Well connected with black veterans associations, he offered to get their help with my plan to have Eddie reburied in Arlington National Cemetery. Joe arranged a meeting with the veterans of the Jackie Robinson Post of the American Legion, and with other black veterans from all over Los Angeles. They were all enthusiastic about having a role in sending a hero to Washington.

About this time a man named Woodfred Jordan called Gloria Long. He was indignant because to date none of the press materials on Sergeant Carter had mentioned anything about the National Guard. Long passed Jordan on to me. As soon as I identified myself, Jordan tore right into me. "How could you let them put out these press releases? They don't say a thing about our contributions. We were the first black National Guard unit in California." On and on he went. "I knew Carter," he said. "We worked together. We started with nothing in Los Angeles, and we trained and built Guard units in San Bernardino and San Diego. We made history." After the war he and Sergeant Carter had been assigned by the Army as instructors in the first black National Guard units to be organized in California. "What Carter did in Germany was a spontaneous act," Jordan continued, "but what we did in Los Angeles was real engineering." Though I was miffed at Jordan's dismissive comment about Sergeant Carter's heroic acts in Germany, I held my tongue. Jordan said he was a master sergeant and he had worked with Eddie Carter and Rance Richardson, who were on loan from the Army to train the National Guard. Here was another piece of the puzzle.

I asked Buddha whether his father had been in the

National Guard. "Oh, yeah," he said, "he used to ride his motorcycle down to the armory on Exposition Boulevard."

When I said, "Why didn't you tell me?" he gave me a blank look. I don't think he remembered it until I brought it up, and that triggered his memory. He didn't recollect very much, but he confirmed that Eddie had had some relationship with the National Guard. The military was obviously important in Eddie's life, but neither Buddha nor Redd recalled their father talking very much about his experiences. They remembered him as a quiet, reserved man who loved to read. He enjoyed the outdoor life as well, and for a time after the war the family lived on a farm near Tacoma, Washington. Buddha recalled that his father demanded respect and disciplined behavior from his sons. But no details about Eddie's time in the National Guard were forthcoming.

As Jordan lived in Alexandria, Virginia, I invited him to the interment ceremony at Arlington. I could talk to him there about his military experiences with my father-in-law. Maybe Eddie's time in the National Guard had something to do with his not being allowed to reenlist.

The process of transferring Eddie's body was terribly complicated. California has fairly difficult requirements for exhuming a body. For example, the state requires that the old casket be destroyed and the remains transferred to a new casket for transport to the new grave site. All of this has to be done in a manner prescribed by the state—and it was not cheap.

I had contacted the Twelfth Armored Division Association after reading about them in *The Hellcats*. Through them I met Andrew Nix, a black veteran who had served in the Seventeenth Armored Infantry Battalion with the Twelfth Armored Division. He never met Eddie, but he was there at the front where Eddie had served. Initially, Nix had been with an all-black port battalion assigned to loading and unloading ships. When the call for combat volunteers came, he became one of the 2,221 black servicemen accepted for combat duty. Nix won a Combat Infantry Badge for his service. Upon returning home he became a funeral director in Philadelphia. I explained our problem with Eddie's reburial, and Andrew Nix immediately came to our assistance. "Don't worry. I'll take care of the casket," he said. "I'll get him a Bates casket, the best."

Mr. Nix went into high gear. He made some phone calls and set things up. He arranged for Latney Funeral Home to pick up the casket when it arrived in Washington. As it turned, out Mr. Nix had a good friend, Thomas Higginbotham, who was the deputy director at Arlington National Cemetery. Not only did Higginbotham help with setting up the reinterment ceremony, but he also made available a reception room for the guests, where we could celebrate Eddie's triumphant reburial. This was an enormous help because the number of people who could be admitted to the Medal of Honor ceremony was severely limited, but I could invite many more to the reception at Arlington.

Meanwhile, in Los Angeles, I was working with the Angelus Funeral Home people to make the arrangements for a community tribute to Sergeant Carter and to ensure that the remains got to Washington in time for the reinterment. The Medal of Honor ceremony was set for Monday, January 13, and the reinterment would be the following day. The big community send-off in Los Angeles was set for Saturday, January 11.

People came from all over for the community celebration. What was most moving for me was to see all the veterans, many of them quite elderly, who attended. There was row after row of them. They were wearing their old uniforms, some of them bedecked with ribbons and medals, and some sporting berets. Among them were representatives of the 761st Tank Battalion, the Tuskegee Airmen, the Buffalo Soldiers Association, Women in the Military Service, the Chappie James Post of the American Legion, the Hispanic American Airborne Association, the Inglewood Post of the Veterans of Foreign Wars, and Jackie Robinson Post No. 252. Many of them wept openly with joy and sadness—joy that Eddie was finally getting the Medal of Honor, which honored them as well, and sadness that he was not there to know it.

The ceremony was almost over when suddenly in came State Senator Dianne Watson. She bolted through

Pallbearers from Jackie Robinson Post 252 escort Sergeant Carter's casket to a hearse in Los Angeles.

the doors and came up front and took the mike. She had heard about Sergeant Carter, she said, and she wanted to honor him by having a "Sergeant Carter Day" at the state capitol in Sacramento, with a ceremony in the Assembly chambers and the family present to receive the state's recognition of him as a hero. I was surprised and, at first, doubtful. But she proved to be true to her word, and the very next month she did sponsor a series of events honoring Sergeant Carter at the state capitol.

Following the community ceremony at Angelus Funeral Home, we went outside into a sunny day and the veterans gave a traditional twenty-one-gun salute. The honor guard, members of the Jackie Robinson Post, then loaded the casket into the waiting hearse and slowly drove away. We had done it. We had reintroduced Eddie to his community. We had let people know that many years ago one of their heroes had been taken away from them, but he was back now and he was being recognized by the White House as a hero to the whole nation.

CHAPTER TWO

HONORING HEROES

The presentation ceremony at the White House would be exciting, but the events leading up to it were very stressful. We had to ship the body to Arlington on Friday, have the community memorial in Los Angeles on Saturday, and then get the whole family, including Mildred, ready to go to Washington for Monday's ceremony at the White House and the reinternment on Tuesday.

Redd and Karen came, and I invited Fred Scott, former husband of Mildred's daughter, Iris. Mildred, Buddha, our teenagers Corey and Santalia, and I were accompanied by a protocol officer, Captain Nguyen, who had flown with us from Los Angeles. When we arrived at the White House there were Secret Service people everywhere. I gave the kids a stern look. "Be on your best behavior," I hissed. "Don't do anything. Don't go anywhere." They responded with looks of angelic innocence, which worried me even more.

The ceremony was held in the East Room. It was packed with cabinet members, senators and members of

Congress, military brass, and family members and friends. The dignitaries included Secretary of Defense William Perry, Secretary Jesse Brown of the Veterans Administration, General Colin Powell, and General John Shalikashvili of the Joint Chiefs of Staff.

We stood as the ceremony began with a military band playing "God Bless America." The Medal of Honor recipients were escorted onto the stage and then President Clinton entered as the band played "Hail to the Chief." Was I excited! Standing just a few feet away was the President of the United States, and my husband, who had been whisked away earlier, was on the stage with him.

President Clinton spoke about the significance of the occasion and the men being honored. "Fifty-two years ago on an August day," he said, "Harry Truman stood where I stand now and awarded twenty-eight Medals of Honor to veterans of World War II in the largest such ceremony ever held." President Truman, he continued, said those recipients were a great cross-section of the United States. "But that day something was missing. . . . No African American who deserved the Medal of Honor for his service in World War II received it. Today we fill the gap in that picture and give a group of heroes who also loved peace but adapted themselves to war the tribute that has always been their due."

A gap in U.S. history *was* being filled—too late, unfortunately, for the men who died, but not too late for the succeeding generations of Americans to learn something.

In addition to Sergeant Carter, the President awarded the Medal of Honor to six men, only one of whom, Vernon J. Baker, was still living. Family members were to receive the awards for the deceased men. All but one of the seven, Ruben Rivers, had been awarded the Distinguished Service Cross. Rivers was awarded a Silver Star, the third-highest award for valor.

These seven men are among "the bravest of the brave," the President said. "Each of them distinguished himself with extraordinary valor, in the famous words, 'at the risk of his life, above and beyond the call of duty.'"

Staff Sergeant Ruben Williams served with the famous all-black 761st Tank Battalion, the Black Panthers. In November 1944, his tank hit a mine while advancing toward the town of Guebling in France. Severely wounded in the leg, Sergeant Rivers refused medical treatment and instead took command of another tank. He continued fighting for three more days while repeatedly refusing morphine or evacuation. "I see 'em, we'll fight 'em," he radioed in as his tank advanced on enemy positions. While providing cover fire to other tanks that had come under attack, his tank was hit. Sergeant Rivers was killed and his crew wounded. He was recommended for a Medal of Honor by his commanding officer, but no action was taken at the time.

As he was leading a task force in France in December 1944, First Lieutenant Charles L. Thomas's scout car was hit by intense enemy fire, and he suffered multiple wounds. Despite the severity of his injuries, Lieutenant Thomas directed the emplacement of antitank guns, which began to effectively return fire. He then thoroughly briefed a junior officer on enemy gun positions and the general situation before allowing himself to be evacuated for medical care.

While acting as lead scout in an action to secure a vital bridgehead near Lippoldsberg, Germany, in April 1945, Private First Class Willy James was the first to draw enemy fire. He was pinned down for more than an hour. He studied the enemy's positions in detail, and eventually managed to get back to his unit, where he used the information he had obtained to help plan a counterattack. He then volunteered to lead the charge against the enemy and point out targets. While going to the aid of his fatally wounded platoon leader, Private James was killed by a German machine gunner.

In March 1943, Private George Watson was aboard a ship near New Guinea that was repeatedly attacked by enemy bombers. When the ship started sinking and had to be abandoned, Private Watson, instead of saving himself, stayed in the water and helped pull several soldiers who could not swim to a life raft. Exhausted by his exertion, he was pulled down by the suction of the sinking ship and drowned.

When advancing German troops stormed into the Italian village of Sommocolinia and drove out the American forces in December 1944, First Lieutenant John R.

Fox volunteered to remain with an observation post force on the second floor of a house near the town. He directed defensive artillery fire in an effort to stop the enemy advance. As the Germans came closer and closer and finally entered the house from which he was watching the German advance, Lieutenant Fox directed that U.S. artillery target his own position. "There are more of them than there are of us," he said. When U.S. troops recaptured the town, Lieutenant Fox's body was found among some one hundred dead German soldiers.

"Edward Carter," the President said, "was crossing an open field in Germany when he was wounded five times. But Staff Sergeant Carter continued to advance, and when eight enemy tried to capture him, he killed six, took two prisoner, and brought them back for interrogation. In the face of overwhelming danger [he] never wavered." President Clinton also noted that Sergeant Carter repeatedly, though unsuccessfully, requested combat duty. "When his request was finally granted it was at the cost of his sergeant's stripes, because an African American was not allowed to command white troops. Today these injustices are behind us."

The seventh and only living Medal of Honor recipient was First Lieutenant Vernon Baker. In April 1945, Lieutenant Baker was a platoon leader in the all-black Ninety-second Infantry Division fighting in Italy. Baker led his platoon in an advance up a hill toward a German stronghold. With his M1 rifle Baker killed two Germans in a bunker and another German who had thrown a hand grenade that failed to explode. Continuing to advance into a canyon alone, Baker used a grenade to blast open the hidden entrance of a German dugout. Dashing inside, he killed two more Germans. When Baker's white commanding officer left to get reinforcements (which never came), Baker rallied his troops to continue fighting. In all, Baker wiped out three enemy machine-gun nests, an observer post, and a dugout.

Now seventy-seven years old, his eyes filled with tears, Vernon Baker stepped forward to have the Medal of Honor placed around his neck by the President. Clinton said he was very moved upon reading about Vernon Baker's creed in life in a newspaper. "He was asked how he bore up under the lack of respect and dignity and honor after all these years. And he said, 'Give respect before you expect it, treat people the way you want to be treated, remember the mission, set the example, keep going.' These are words for all of us."

"Today," the President continued, "America is profoundly thankful for the patriotism and the nobility of these men, and for the example they set, which helped us to find the way to become a more just, more free nation. They helped America to become more worthy of them and more true to its ideals."

I valued the President's remarks, but I could not help but recall that U.S. government agencies were actively spying on black civil rights activists as potential subversives in the years following World War II. The struggle for

*President Clinton presents the Congressional Medal of Honor
to Sergeant Carter's son Edward III at a White House ceremony,
January 13, 1997. Seated at right is Vernon Baker, also
a Congressional Medal of Honor repicient.*

black freedom was not applauded by all, and the injustices
of the past were not entirely behind us.

After a photo session with the President, we were
taken to the Hall of Heroes. There they unveiled pictures
of the seven new black Medal of Honor winners. What
began just over eight months ago with a phone call from

President Clinton greets Mildred Carter, Eddie's widow, at the Medal of Honor ceremony. At left is William "Redd" Carter and his wife, Karen.

General Colin Powell with Sergeant Carter's grandson Corey at the Medal of Honor ceremony.

Gloria Long had finally come to this moving conclusion. And while no ghosts from Eddie's past blighted the day, I still had unanswered questions. Why had this distinguished soldier not been allowed back into the Army? Why was the family silent about what had happened to him? I pondered these questions as we prepared for the burial at Arlington the next day.

Tuesday was beautiful but cold as Eddie's casket was placed on a horse-drawn caisson with an honor guard

Honor guard escorts caisson at Arlington National Cemetery.

escorting it. The family rode in cars that followed the caisson to the grave site.

It was all very solemn and impressive. A formation of fighter planes flew over to honor Eddie; an honor guard fired its rifles to salute him. The chaplain read some appropriate lines of scripture as we sat there. But for me it was an emotional letdown. Gloria Long had asked if some of the media could be invited to the reinterment. Not realizing how stressful the media's presence would be, I had said yes. Cameras were flashing in our faces, and the press was everywhere. We hadn't had time to deal with our emotions alone, and as a family we didn't have the time to absorb this moment. Still, despite the media, I felt Eddie's presence as I sat there. I wanted to say to him, "This is where you should be. This is what you deserve. This is where you should have been all along."

A reception for all the guests followed the burial ceremony. Vernon Baker was there along with Andrew Nix and other veterans from the Twelfth Armored Division. This was when I met Russell Blair, who had been one of Eddie's white commanding officers. A soft-spoken man from Texas, Blair seemed sincerely pleased that Eddie had finally gotten the Medal of Honor. He told me how impressed he was with Eddie. "He was a real soldier," Blair said. "He soldiered twenty-four hours a day. He was one of the best soldiers I've ever seen."

And there was Woodfred Jordan, the irate soldier who told me about Eddie's involvement in the National Guard.

A slight, skinny man who roared like he was six-foot-six, he loved to talk and immediately launched into stories about his days in the National Guard, and how he and Eddie and another soldier named Rance Richardson used to play cards at night. I pulled him aside and said, "Mr. Jordan, we'll talk about all the things you guys used to do later. Right now I want to show you something." I showed him some of the photographs I had found in Mildred's trunk. "That's me!" he shouted. And it was. "That's Richardson," he said pointing to another figure. The photos were of the National Guard units he and Eddie and Richardson had trained after the war. Jordan went on to say that his wife and Richardson's wife were twin sisters. He told me that Eddie and Mildred used to socialize with the four of them in Los Angeles. They often went over to Richardson's house to play cards. "Yeah," he said. "Carter smoked a cigar and he seemed to be on top of the world. And they were watching him. He knew they were watching him."

"Who was watching him, and why?" I asked. Jordan suddenly became cagey. He didn't know, he said.

As I listened to Jordan I realized that every time a piece of the puzzle seemed to fall into place it also raised more questions. Perhaps we had accomplished a mission in coming to Washington, but our journey—my journey—was far from over.

CHAPTER THREE

LIFE IN INDIA AND CHINA

Although I had not anticipated it, the Medal of Honor and reinterment ceremonies in January 1997 were only the beginning of a whirlwind of events that would continue through most of the year. From Valley Forge to Sacramento to Fort Huachuca, Arizona, we went out to black communities, civic organizations, and veterans groups to participate in ceremonies honoring the Medal of Honor recipients. We were called upon to be the stand-ins for the deceased husbands, fathers, grandfathers, and uncles whose belated recognition won them a prideful place in the hearts of many people.

Despite this demanding round of events, I had not forgotten the unanswered questions that remained in the back of my mind. Why had Eddie been barred from reenlisting in the Army? What did Woodfred Jordan mean when he said Eddie was being watched while he was in the National Guard? I couldn't get over the feeling that trouble might be brewing for us somewhere. A journalist acquaintance suggested that I could obtain government records through the Freedom of Information Act that might shed light on any problems Eddie had had while in the Army. I submitted a request to the Federal Bureau of Investigation. Months later I got a form letter saying that the FBI had a tremendous backlog of requests, that they were understaffed, and that my request had not yet been assigned for initial review. "In view of our current workload," the letter ended, "you may expect a delay of several months." That did not sound very hopeful.

In the meantime, I was also piecing together the story of Eddie's rather unusual childhood.

Eddie was born in Los Angeles on May 26, 1916. His father, Edward A. Carter, a small, dark-skinned man with a searching gaze, was an evangelist and missionary with the Holiness Church. Though not a physically large man, the force of the elder Carter's personality and his powerful oratorical skills made his presence loom large to those who knew him. Eddie's mother was Mary Stuart Carter, a young Anglo-Indian woman from Calcutta. Her family had come to Los Angeles, where she met Carter. She was also a missionary with the Holiness Church. Two other children, William and Miriam, were born to the couple after Eddie. Through passport records, letters, and church documents I pieced together the story of this unusual family and its remarkable journey to India and, later, China.

Eddie's father was born in 1877 in Trinidad, Colorado.

Eddie Carter with his mother, Mary Carter, 1916.

He lived in Colorado Springs, Kansas City, and El Paso before arriving in Los Angeles. Mary Wilhelmina Stuart, Eddie's mother, was some twenty years younger than his father. She was variously described as "colored," "East Indian," or "Hindu." Her father was an Englishman and her mother was from India.

In Los Angeles, Eddie's father worked as a cook for wealthy families. A first marriage ended when his wife died in a traffic accident. At some point the elder Carter underwent a powerful conversion experience, which hit him with such intensity that he threw a pot of soup he was cooking into the air. The experience also launched him on a lifelong career as an evangelist. He soon developed a reputation for his colorful and powerful rhetoric. One witness praised his thunderous sermons as a "wonderful combination of scriptural reference and great emotional enthusiasm . . . not expository preaching but more experiential preaching."

His style was so effective that it even won him a blessing in the form of his marriage to Mary Stuart on May 2, 1915. Speaking in church years later, Mary described his effect on her. "When I first came to this country from Calcutta, East India, I joined the Catholic Church, intending to become a nun. Later I became a Seventh-Day Adventist, but still I never knew God in peace. I met Mr. Carter, and through his life and teaching I found Jesus in his saving power."

Mary was only a girl when she married Evangelist Carter—and like many younger women who marry older men, she may have felt in awe of him—but over the next ten years of marriage she grew into a self-confident woman who was also a powerful speaker. She told of having a vision of "a vast body of water, and beyond were a great multitude of Hindus." Her "vision" may have been the genesis of an irresistible calling that propelled them to India, where they hoped to "establish holiness." They were not the only ones called. The Holiness Church had a program of establishing missions in foreign lands. Already it had missions in South America and Palestine.

Whatever the genesis of the move, in early May 1925, some 235 people gathered at the church mission hall for

Evangelist Edward A. Carter Sr.

an emotional farewell service, and the Carter family set sail for India aboard the steamer *Korea Maru*. A passport photograph showed the family at that time. The elder Carter was dressed formally in a jacket, vest, and tie. Beside him stood Mary Carter, a lovely young woman in a modest dress with a wide collar, her hair pulled straight back. Eddie Jr., his eyes somewhat veiled, stood close to

Passport photograph of the Carter family taken in Los Angeles shortly before they departed for India in 1925. Left to right: Mary Carter, Eddie, Miriam, William, Evangelist Carter. (Courtesy U.S. Passport Office)

her, just behind her left shoulder. Miriam, with a ribbon in her hair, was placed in front between her parents, while William stood behind his father's right shoulder.

After a stopover in San Francisco, the ship arrived in Honolulu, where the Carters posted a letter to their church. They were thankful, they wrote, that none of them had gotten seasick "while others are sick all around us." An appeal for divine help was promptly answered: "We had some very rough weather for a few days and nights so Sister Carter and I spoke to Father about it and

that settled it." They also reported holding a service—
"a good meeting," they thought—on the boat the previous Sunday. Eddie would have just turned nine years old;
William was seven and Miriam was four.

On June 25, 1925, some six weeks after their departure,
following stops at Yokohama, Shanghai, and Hong Kong,
the family finally walked down the gangplank in Calcutta,
a congested city then under British colonial rule. They
arrived with only 150 rupees to their name. They spent
the first night at the Metropolitan Hotel at a cost of 20
rupees and registered with the American consul the next
day. With the help of a friend they found rooms on Dhur-
rumtollah Street and a landlord willing to wait for pay-
ment of the 150-rupee rent until they received funds from
home. On the following night they held their first meeting
for potential converts. "We have fired the first gun for
holiness, so our work and your work has begun in Calcutta," they reported.

The funds they hoped to receive would not be great.
In June, the church treasurer reported that only $6.25 had
been collected to support the Carters' missionary work.
The monthly donation fluctuated, reaching a peak of
$89.46 in March 1926. It was apparent that the Carters
would have to find support among their new converts in
India.

Shortly after the Carters arrived, Calcutta was
drenched with monsoon rains, heavy downpours that
often caused flooding. The rains would be followed by a

dry season that all too often resulted in drought and famine. As if the contrasts of flood and drought were not enough, India was beset by frequent epidemics. The most recent one, in 1924, had killed over 300,000 people. Calcutta was a city of extremes of wealth and social circumstance, where many lived in hovels while others lived in palaces. It offered fertile ground for missionaries. Hunger, disease, and despair made thousands of Indians ready to welcome any message of hope.

After only a month in Calcutta the Carters were having great success in winning converts. "The rain does not stop us or the people from coming out to meetings," Evangelist Carter wrote. Mary preached at one meeting at which eight souls were converted. In all some sixty-five converts to Christianity had been gained. The meetings were sometimes held at the Thornborn Methodist Episcopal Church, but this was only temporary. "We are hoping to have a place soon which will be the First Holiness Church of Calcutta," Carter reported. "Don't you feel like shouting?"

All was going well. The family had moved into new housing that was made available free of charge. The children were also well. William had suffered from some kind of infection in his legs, but this cleared up. "Sister Carter and I got right down on our knees and prayed through on his healing." Evangelist Carter's sole complaint was that they had gotten only one letter from home since arriving. "News from home is scarce and you will never know how lonesome a person can get in India in a city of a million inhabitants, until you have been here."

Received into the homes of several Indian families, Carter reported observations he thought would interest the folks back home and give them a sense of the great work required in India.

The people are of every shade of color from white to very black; some have red hair, some blond hair and some with their hair shaved off, with just a little queue hanging down their backs. They think that when Jesus comes, He will take them by this queue and lift them up to heaven. The people here wear ankle bracelets, nose rings, ear rings, nose jewels, arm bracelets and rings on their toes; so you see it will mean something for them to give all this up. We will have to teach them to wear clothing as many only wear a cloth about their loins. One of the great problems that confront us is the animosity between the Anglo-Indian and the real Indian. The Anglo-Indian has a white father or mother and is very proud of this extraction, and feels the full-blood Indian is his inferior and vice versa. They have separate churches and missions, but we are preaching and God is getting them together.

It is interesting that Evangelist Carter focused on the "great problem" posed by race mixing and color consciousness among Indians. Perhaps this was an expression of his sensibility as a black man (or, as he preferred, an "Ethiopian") raised in racially segregated and color-conscious America. Because they were a mixed couple, and because Mary Carter herself was Anglo-Indian, Evangelist Carter may have felt that they were well suited to oppose separation based on color and caste, that they could succeed in bringing people together.

In any case, their missionary work was phenomenally successful, reportedly gaining a thousand converts within a matter of months. They also secured a building in which to house their Holiness Church mission. A photograph of it, along with the Carters and some of their converts, appeared in the *Pentecost,* the church newspaper.

Through 1926 their work grew and their household arrangement became more complex and costly. The children were enrolled in the mission school, and the family had hired a man and a woman to help with domestic chores and the children. Eddie was very close to his mother, but his relationship with his father was difficult. Years later, Eddie said that as a child in India he couldn't get along with his father, that sometimes his father beat him, and twice Eddie ran away from home. Eddie dreamed of escaping to another kind of life. His family lived near a military post, and it was here that Eddie's lifelong fascination with the military took root. He said he once had a vision of a visit by a spirit that told him he would become a great warrior, that he would be wounded many times, but that he would survive so long as he protected his chest.

AND THEY WERE ALL FILLED WITH THE HOLY SPIRIT

The PENTECOST

HOLINESS UNTO THE LORD

HE THAT WINNETH SOULS IS WISE

42nd YEAR   WHOLE NUMBER 1360

PUBLISHED WEEKLY   LOS ANGELES, CALIFORNIA,   January 6, 1926.

of Indians who are educated and work in offices as bookkeepers and typists.

THE OASIS
Part I.
A Desert Scene.

A great arid waste of fine white sand, everywhere, sand, glistening, gleaming sand. No animal or vegetable life is visible anywhere; as far as the eye can see is a great sea of white hot sand. In the midst of this desolate scene a lone man is trudging along under the mid-day semi-tropical sun. The canteen hanging from his belt was drained of the last few precious drops of water the day before. His bloodshot and aching eyes search the horizon in vain for some signs of vegetation which would indicate water. The swollen tongue and parched lips bring intense agony, while the mind is absorbed with the thought of water. In his mind's eye he can see the springs and wells of crystal water that he has drank from in other days, when the desert was unknown to him. In his imagination he

A group of converts in Calcutta, India. Missionaries E. A. Carter and Wife in the center, front row.

The above picture was taken in of. is the use of the betelnut. lime and

Front page of the Pentecost, *January 6, 1926, showing Mr. and Mrs. Carter, seated center with daughter Miriam, in front of Holiness Church in Calcutta with some of their converts. (Courtesy Wesleyan Archives)*

While Eddie entertained thoughts of being a soldier, both Edward and Mary Carter were busy with the nightly meetings of their missionary work. Though not always well herself, Mary helped heal a sick woman through prayer, Carter Sr., reported. Aside from health problems and ever-present financial worries, there was no hint of any other difficulties in the letters and reports they sent back home to Los Angeles. Then, suddenly it seems, their household was disrupted.

In the April 20, 1927, edition of the *Pentecost,* among the committee and board notes, in small type at the back of the issue, I found a brief report to the Board of Elders. "Letters were read from Brother Carter stating that his wife had eloped with Irwin H. James, taking their little girl with them; and stating in a heartbreaking way his desire to find and forgive her, and his surprise at what his wife and friend had done. Also letters from the American Consul of Calcutta, India, and the Government at Washington. Prayers offered for Brother Carter." Carter wired for financial help when he learned that not only had the church's general secretary and treasurer run off with his wife, he had also absconded with the church's funds. Mary didn't return, although Carter subsequently gained custody of Miriam.

Because William and Miriam were so young, they were probably less affected by this turn of events, but the loss of his mother devastated Eddie. Further, the relationship between Eddie and his father, strained during the best of times, was now irreversibly damaged. In fact, I think Eddie tried to be the opposite of his father. Missionaries, in Eddie's view, weren't hardworking or courageous men. His dreams of being a soldier only grew. There would never be a reconciliation between Eddie and the elder Carter.

Meanwhile, though his father may have been devastated by the loss of his wife as well, he had to carry on. By the middle of the summer of 1927, Evangelist Carter had planned to return to the United States. He applied for a second passport. This passport, issued on August 12, included his three children, but not Mary Carter, and tellingly depicts, in its photograph, Eddie standing farthest away from his father. On the application the elder Carter stated that he intended to return to the United States within one month. He secured passage on the *Korea Maru*, the same ship that brought his family from the United States to India, but unexpectedly, on September 9, he found himself and his three children cast off the boat in Shanghai, China.

During what was to be the journey home, young William suddenly took ill with a high fever. The ship's doctor suspected it was typhoid fever. Dismayed, Evangelist Carter prayed fervently for William's recovery, but the fever only got worse. When the ship reached Shanghai, the family was required to disembark or be forcibly removed.

Fabled in the nineteenth century for its opium dens and prostitution, and as the unsought destination of many a hapless sailor, Shanghai in 1927 was a thriving commercial and financial center whose busy port connected China to Europe and North America. It was the most cosmopolitan and westernized city in China, with a large resident European population. Sections of Shanghai, especially along the Bund, its famous waterfront thoroughfare and location of many hotels, banks, and other commercial establishments, looked more like a European capital than a Chinese city. Fortunately for Evangelist Carter, the large European population meant the presence of a general hospital where William could be treated.

Carter settled his family in a hotel to wait and pray. "My son Edward did not think William was going to die," he wrote to the church in Los Angeles. William remained in serious condition; the doctors said that he might need to be hospitalized for forty to sixty days. "Daddy, maybe God wants you to stay in Shanghai," Eddie said to his father. "Would you if he wanted you to?" The elder Carter decided that "God was trying to speak to me but I had a hard fight to say *yes* to Jesus, but William never began to get well until I did say *yes* to Jesus."

Shortly after arriving in Shanghai, Evangelist Carter met a Chinese Christian who helped him find a home for his family, and he began preaching to Chinese people through a translator and any Europeans who would listen. As William's health began to improve, Carter befriended other missionaries and was invited to preach at various meetings, including a series of evangelistic meetings held at the Chinese YMCA.

For five weeks I labored at the Chinese Y.M.C.A. to a packed house; many times the people could not get into the auditorium. From there I went into the London Mission Church and then to the Christian

Alliance Church. Wherever I was people flocked by the hundreds, and standing room was always at a premium.

Despite his troubles in Calcutta, Carter had not lost his fervor or brilliance as an evangelist. Holiness Church officials in Los Angeles continued to support him financially as he established a missionary venture in China that would become astonishingly successful. Enrolling the children in an American Holiness school, he threw himself wholeheartedly into this new calling, traveling to other cities and taking his message into the Chinese countryside. He based himself in Shanghai, where, by 1928, three Holiness missions had been established. He wrote home that souls were being saved by the hundreds and thousands.

Evangelist Carter attributed his success in part to being a black missionary in China. He recounted a visit to the northwest where a local Chinese commander told him, "We are glad you came to China. We need a man like you." Carter commented: "This is the time *color counts.* I can go where the white missionaries cannot go. I am trying to show them the oneness of God's people and hundreds have accepted Jesus Christ." With antiforeign (meaning primarily anti-European) sentiment growing in China, Evangelist Carter was not identified with the "foreign devils." In many areas he was hailed as the "Black Evangelist." His success, however, was not always well received by white missionaries. "The foreign missionaries are unable to go into the places where God has given your humble servant an open door," he reported. "Some of them say they have been here thirty or forty years and have not been able to do the things reported to you. Some have even said I should go to America. It seems they are becoming envious."

Other observers confirmed Evangelist Carter's success. A "white businessman" writing in the *China Courier* said that "great crowds were assembled to hear this man." Carter won praise from Jennie V. Hughes of Bethel Mission, who wrote to the *Pentecost* that "The Chinese from the first opened their hearts to him." Once when Evangelist Carter protested that he was also a foreigner, an American, she wrote that a Chinese convert "put his arms around [Carter] and replied, 'Oh, no, you are not a foreigner. You are just our brother.'"

Carter happily reported that Eddie and William were involved in the mission work. "Edward and William are saved and sanctified," he wrote, "and are a great help in the singing in our evening prayer meetings, and how they do pray for the people!" He said people sometimes called Eddie "the young preacher."

Beyond his reputation as a powerful orator, even through an interpreter, Carter also became known for having the gift of healing through prayer. He acknowledged the importance of healing when he wrote that "God is not only saving and sanctifying souls here in China, but He is also healing, and because of this, many

souls are accepting Him as their personal Savior." Healing the sick through prayer was a common practice at
meetings, and Carter was sometimes called by wealthy
families to pray for a sick relative. In one report home he
described how he was called by a Chinese family to pray
for their teenage daughter, Myrtle, who was suffering with
typhoid fever. The doctors had described her case as very
dangerous. Her situation did not look hopeful, and an
intense bedside prayer meeting was held, led by Carter.
"We surely prayed a hole right through the skies to the
throne of God. The doctor was dismissed, and thank God
we can say, Myrtle is healed, and they are planning a
thanksgiving service at the Cantonese church just as soon
as Myrtle is stronger."

Although Evangelist Carter's reputation was growing,
it was a difficult and dangerous time to be in China.
China was burdened by a legacy of European and American imperialist intervention dating back to the nineteenth
century. After China's humiliating defeat in the Opium
Wars—stemming from attempts by the Chinese government to stop the British from importing opium into
China—Europeans gained control of key Chinese cities,
including Hong Kong and Shanghai. Shanghai was
divided into a number of "concessions," international set-
tlements of resident foreigners (and a few wealthy Chinese) protected by troops of their own governments.
Added to this was a growing civil war in the 1920s
between communist forces led by Mao Tse-tung and a

right-wing Nationalist Army under Generalissimo Chiang Kai-shek, combined with continuing violence by gangs and warlords and the ever-present threat of famine, all of which caused widespread death and destruction and tore Chinese society apart. The elder Carter and his children arrived in Shanghai not long after a bloody massacre of communists by the Nationalist forces, and the fighting continued in other areas throughout the countryside. It was a time of enormous suffering for the Chinese people. To the Chinese Nationalists and wealthy classes, Carter's success among ordinary Chinese—where so many foreign missionaries had failed—and his status as an American connected with an American Christian church made him a man of some interest.

It was only a matter of months after his arrival in China that Evangelist Carter was introduced to a wealthy Chinese family that was linked to both American Christianity and the Chinese Nationalists. "We were invited to the home of a very rich Chinese to dinner," he reported. "I could scarcely find a more accomplished family. The children had studied in America, and came out of school with high honors." Carter did not name the family, but his description suggests this may have been his first meeting with the Soong family, a wealthy and influential Christian family in Shanghai. He would have been introduced to them by other missionaries, as the family was well known in the missionary community and active in spreading the gospel.

Sterling Seagrave's fascinating and best-selling book *The Soong Dynasty* (1985) brought this family to the attention of a new generation of U.S. readers, and in 1997 *The Soong Sisters,* a fictionalized film about the three sisters, was released. Charlie Soong, the patriarch of the family, whose Chinese name was Han Chiao-shun, was born into a merchant family in China's Kwangtung Province. In 1879, Charlie, like many Chinese, emigrated to the United States in search of a better life. Unlike most Chinese immigrants, however, he succeeded, with the aid of white Christian benefactors, in gaining an education at Trinity College in Durham, North Carolina, and Vanderbilt University in Nashville, Tennessee. His chief benefactor was Julian Carr, who made his money in tobacco and was a founder of Duke University. Under the influence of a Methodist minister, Charlie also converted to Christianity. Along the way he dropped his Chinese name. Returning to China, Charlie worked for a time as a Methodist missionary and teacher, then he launched his first business, a Bible-publishing business in Shanghai, set up with financial assistance from wealthy Chinese Christians and the help of Julian Carr. His business ventures became enormously successful, making Charlie rich and powerful. He used his wealth to support the growing nationalist movement in China, and his Bible-publishing business became a cover for printing nationalist literature.

In 1887, Charlie Soong married Ni Kwei-tseng, the daughter of a wealthy Chinese Christian family. The couple had three daughters and three sons. The children established the Soong "dynasty." Two of his sons became financiers, and the oldest, T. V. Soong, was at various times finance minister, foreign minister, and prime minister in the government of Chiang Kai-shek. The daughters were even more interesting. Educated, shrewd women, they were powerful individuals, although in China their power had to be expressed through their connection with men. The oldest, Ai-ling, considered the family mastermind, was educated at Wesleyan College, a Methodist college for women in Macon, Georgia. Known for her financial cunning, she married the wealthy H. H. Kung and helped him become finance minister and minister of industry, commerce, and labor in Chiang Kai-shek's government. Ai-ling was also linked with the dark side of Chinese society, the powerful gangs that were involved in the opium trade and other criminal activity.

The second daughter, Ching-ling, also educated at Wesleyan, married Sun Yat-sen, the father of the Chinese nationalist movement and hero to the Chinese people. After Sun's death, Ching-ling joined forces with Mao Tse-tung and became vice-chairman of the People's Republic of China after the communist victory in 1949. The youngest daughter, Mei-ling, also attended Wesleyan, graduated from Wellesley College, and married Chiang Kai-shek in December 1927. She was China's first lady until the communist victory, when she and her husband and their supporters fled to Taiwan. Known as the power behind the throne of Nationalist China, Madame Chiang, elegant and charming, became extremely popular in the American media and helped solidify U.S. support for the repressive regime of her husband.

Also in the Soong household, employed as a German language tutor, was Marie Adele Westerhold, a pretty young German woman with bright red hair. In February 1928, Westerhold and Carter married.

I knew from Eddie's family that there was a second "Mary" Carter. We had received news of her death in 1987 in Germany from Elsa Schulz, who cared for her in her last years. Marie Westerhold had been born in Bremen, Germany, in 1906. With the help of an aunt in China, she had left her home in Germany to serve as a missionary in China. She supported herself by working as a tutor. When she married Carter, she was twenty-one years old; he was fifty-one. What brought them together I can only surmise, but they worked together in China as missionaries until the Japanese invaded in 1937, and she remained devoted to Carter—whom she called "Daddy"— until he died in 1966.

What became of the first Mary Carter? A registration application filed by Carter on November 1, 1927, with the U.S. Consulate General in Shanghai only deepened the mystery. The form had a line for indicating when the applicant's prior marital relation was terminated. The date,

February 1927, was entered on that line. Elsewhere the form asked for the date of the prior marriage and spouse's name, and this was followed by the notation that "Mary Wilhelmina is now deceased." When and how the first Mary Carter died has never been explained.

For Eddie, his father's sudden marriage to Mary Westerhold must have been very disturbing. It was only a year since Eddie had experienced the traumatic separation from his mother. He never saw his mother again, and apparently she died in India. Now he was expected to accept a white stranger, who was hardly more than a girl herself, as a replacement for his mother. It was an impossible situation. Mary Westerhold's presence only further deepened Eddie's alienation from his father.

Meanwhile, the military situation in China, the civil war between warlords, Nationalists, and communists, was growing ever more dangerous. Writing in May 1928, Carter said, "They are still fighting a few hundred miles north of us, and there have within the last few days been killed twenty to thirty thousand soldiers, and those that are taken prisoners are being put in the front ranks of the battle line and shot down, while some of the officers are taken and their heads cut off. Two more missionaries have paid the price of their lives." He said that twice a month he visited the Chinese Red Cross hospital to minister to the nurses and wounded soldiers. Shanghai, for the moment spared from the fighting, was a center of "sin and filth" that waylaid American Marines and even some missionaries. Writing in the September 26, 1928, issue of the *Standard Bearer of Bible Holiness* (the new name of the *Pentecost*), Carter said he believed that despite the worsening conditions, the Nationalist government in power was trying to establish a "real government" for China.

In the summer of 1929, Evangelist Carter moved his family into the French concession in Shanghai. Living in the international community was considered safer than living in the Chinese part of the city, and Carter may have been urged by some of his Chinese Christian friends who also lived there to move. He settled in a residence on Route de Sieyes. According to Seagrave's book, *The Soong Dynasty*, this is the same street on which the Kung family had a house. The Chiang and Kung families were very close.

In a letter from the French concession on July 29, Evangelist Carter reported that things were happening "thick and fast" in China. Radical students were holding demonstrations in the streets of Shanghai, and gunfire could be heard in many parts of the city. People were clearing out of the districts where trouble was expected. But in the French concession it was still peaceful. "Where we are living right now," he reported, "we are able to have street meetings right in front of our door." Moreover, Ai-ling Soong—Madame Kung—had offered help.

Madame Kung, the wife of Dr. H. H. Kung, the Minister of Commerce, Industry, and Labor, invited us to hold meetings every Sunday morning at her home. This is a special privilege, that has never been accorded to any of the missionaries or evangelists, and we feel that this door has really been opened to us by the Lord.

Recognizing that Mary Carter also had something to do with this door being opened, this is the first report home in which she is included as a cosigner: "Evangelist and Mrs. E. A. Carter."

By December 1929, Carter, with the help his new wife, had further consolidated his influence with the Soongs. Through them he hoped to secure the conversion of Chiang Kai-shek to Christianity. This would be an enormous religious and political victory.

On December 16, 1929, Carter wrote:

On last Tuesday, the mother-in-law of General Chiang Kai-shek, the president of China, came to our house for me to pray especially for the government at this time. I know you will be glad to know that just a short time ago, General Chiang Kai-shek gave up his idol worship, and his mother-in-law, Mrs. Soong, smashed them to pieces for him, so you see we felt at liberty to pray with her and for General Chiang and the government. [T]he General wrote in a letter to his mother-in-law in his own handwriting, Chinese of course, and Mrs. Soong allowed my wife to read the same, as my wife not only speaks but reads the Chinese language. [S]o we have the words of the General himself that it is the God which we serve that has delivered him out of many trying and difficult situations, and even saved him from being assassinated, and now he says he is going to trust in that God and in His strength. Now let us pray that this general may step right out boldly for Christ and declare that he has accepted Jesus, and if he does this I am sure that one of the greatest troubles that the missionaries have in getting the Gospel to the Chinese will be over. Well, praise God for Jesus!

Securing Chiang Kai-shek's conversion to Christianity was a prize hoped for by many missionaries. Evangelist Carter was uniquely placed to win the prize. Perhaps Carter believed that if Chiang Kai-shek, who controlled the Nationalist Army and the Kuomintang Party, were converted to Christianity, this would be an important step toward bringing peace to China and ending the suffering of the Chinese people. He could not know that even greater suffering was in store for the people in the next decade as Japan brutally tried to subdue China and all of Asia. As for Chiang Kai-shek, he had reasons of his own, beyond spiritual belief, to consider conversion. The United States was a largely Christian nation, and U.S. support was increasingly important in his campaign against Mao Tse-tung's Red Army and, later, the Japanese. To Chiang, Western missionaries were a part of the foreign influence that prostrated and humiliated China. But he understood that sometimes the support of the foreigners was needed in the fight against his enemies, and if the foreigners' God could also help him, then so much the better. And then, unexpectedly, Chiang was to witness a dramatic demonstration of the power of Evangelist Carter's God.

In his most remarkable report from China, Carter described an incident that occurred in January 1930, in which he prayed for the healing of Chiang Kai-shek's young niece, the daughter of Ai-ling Soong and H. H. Kung.

Carter said he was called to Nanking, the Nationalist capital, to pray for Jeanette Kung, who was desperately ill with what was thought to be pneumonia or pleurisy. "There were four of the best doctors that China affords, and yet they could do nothing for this little nine-year-old girl," he wrote. Carter and family members began an impassioned and prolonged prayer session. The next day an X-ray picture revealed that the child's condition had cleared up. "I had the pleasure of witnessing then to these doctors that Jesus Christ, the Great Physician, had made the girl whole."

The healing of Jeanette Kung had a great impact on her family, some of whom immediately sought Carter's help with their own ailments. More important, the episode gave Carter an opportunity to speak to Chiang five years in the military academy, learning military arts and becoming an excellent rifle marksman.

But Eddie could not be contained. A Japanese attack on Shanghai in 1932 found Eddie volunteering to join with Chinese and British forces in resisting the invaders. Pleading that Eddie was underage, his father intervened and got him out of the line of fire after a month on the front lines. Presumably Eddie returned to the academy.

Italy's invasion of Ethiopia in 1935 created another opportunity for Eddie to test the limits of his father's control and find another kind of life. Eddie went to the American consulate in Shanghai and requested to fight against the Italians in Abyssinia. By then Eddie's military academy training and brief combat experience had earned him the rank of lieutenant. The consul was taken aback, and refused this brash request, instead offering to obtain a merchant marine job for Eddie on a freighter. Eddie accepted, and the elder Carter voiced no objection. The boy with the guarded, wounded look in his eyes, the boy who sang in the mission choir, the boy who had been beaten and run away, who was also the boy who had lost the person he loved most dearly, was now a nineteen-year-old young man who would make his own way in the world and find a new life for himself.

Eddie spent the next months on the high seas, traveling to Japan and the Philippines and eventually arriving in Los

Kai-shek about Christianity. At one point in the conversation, with Minister Kung acting as translator, Carter said to Chiang, "Have you peace in your heart, Commander?" "No, not a little bit," was the reply. "That is because of sin," Carter responded. "You have sins in your heart and a sinner cannot have peace. He will be able to take away your sins; then you will find peace in your heart. China needs no more navy, or army, no more guns to kill, no more soldiers that will cause lots of trouble, and not more principles but the Lord Jesus Christ. He can save China from all these troubles." Carter said the general reacted cordially to these admonishments, saying that he would begin to read the Bible.

It is not hard to imagine that the dramatic healing of Jeanette Kung would have deeply impressed Chiang Kai-shek, who was already being lobbied by Madame Soong to convert to Christianity. No doubt he knew of Carter, who had married someone close to the Soong family. There is a story told in our family that Chiang Kai-shek would have preferred that Carter had married a Chinese girl. Chiang wanted to literally and figuratively wed the famous "Black Evangelist" to China, and more specifically the Chinese Nationalists. But in choosing Mary Westerhold, Carter, wittingly or not, achieved a valuable connection with, and yet independence from, a powerful man who demanded unquestioning loyalty. In any case, the meeting between the two men in the wake of the healing episode propelled Chiang to make his decision. In a later report, Carter announced Chiang Kai-shek was baptized in the Soong family home.

Chiang became a practicing Methodist and an ardent reader of the Bible. He was not simply looking for its spiritual messages but also for justification of his actions against his enemies. Puritanical in his outlook, he and Madame Chiang founded the New Life Movement to encourage physical and spiritual cleanliness, and to discourage such practices as smoking, drinking, dancing, permanent hairwaves, gambling, and spitting in the streets. In the name of moral uplift, the New Life Movement concealed the deepening fascism of the Nationalist regime. Chiang would soon emerge as an admirer of Mussolini and Hitler.

CHAPTER FOUR

A WARRIOR COMES OF AGE

While his father was gaining notoriety, Eddie was growing into a robust teenager who loved fishing and hunting. Later he developed a love for sports, including baseball, football, track, and boxing. He had also learned to speak Hindustani, Mandarin Chinese, and some German. He felt at home with Indians, and during his adolescent years he developed a strong identification with the Chinese people. As for an American identity, he knew he was considered a black American, but African-American culture was something with which he would not become intimately acquainted until he lived in Los Angeles in the 1940s. From an early age Eddie displayed a love of adventure and a desire for excitement matched by personal courage that left little room for fear. Like other boys his age, he was in and out of trouble. Apparently in an effort to channel and discipline Eddie's rebellious spirit, his father enrolled him in a Chinese military academy. Chiang Kai-shek, who, of course, had direct ties to Chinese military institutions, including an academy in Shanghai, may have facilitated this transfer. In all, Eddie spent

Angeles. The United States was in the throes of the Great Depression and times were hard for black men seeking work. Eddie found little opportunity and nothing to spark his interest. What did get his attention was news of the civil war in Spain.

In 1936, a democratically elected Republican government in Spain was attacked by right-wing forces under the control of General Francisco Franco. A fierce and bloody conflict soon raged between Loyalist forces defending the republican government and Insurgent forces trying to overthrow it and restore the monarchy. Franco and his troops were heavily supported by German Nazis and Italian Fascists. The Soviet Union supported the republicans, while the United States adopted a noninterventionist stance. The Spanish Civil War, like the Chinese fight against Japanese imperialists, would be recognized by historians as a precursor to World War II.

The war in Spain was on the front pages of newspapers throughout the United States. Eddie, a young man in quest of a meaning for his life, was drawn to the embattled republicans. Using his merchant marine connections he found a ship that took him first to Africa, then to Spain. Soon after his arrival he joined the Loyalist forces.

Hundreds of other young American men volunteered to go to Spain to help the Loyalists, among them some ninety black Americans who fought in integrated units with white volunteers. Unlike Eddie, who was not recruited and who made his own way to Spain, these volunteers arrived in groups and were organized into what became the Abraham Lincoln Brigade. The volunteers were mostly inexperienced, idealistic youths. Given scant training, they were thrown into combat against seasoned troops.

Already trained in the military arts and experienced in combat in China, Eddie was better prepared than most of the volunteers to survive the horrendous conditions of the war. Many volunteers died, both from combat and the harsh conditions they encountered. Eddie himself was wounded. In the incident, which he recounted years later, Eddie was part of a small reconnaissance patrol, the only black person in the group. The patrol was moving fast when suddenly, coming over a rise of land, they ran into a German unit. The Germans opened fire, killing everyone but Eddie. Eddie was hit in the heel, but he managed to roll hand grenades down the slope toward the Germans and escape. Later in the war Eddie was not so lucky. He was captured by Franco's troops and held in a prison camp for several months. Never one to passively accept his fate, Eddie somehow escaped from the camp and rejoined the Loyalist forces.

In all, Eddie was in Spain for two and a half years, when his unit was finally forced to retreat into France. By early 1939 the Loyalists faced a bitter defeat as Franco's troops, backed by his Fascist and Nazi allies, overwhelmed the republican defenders.

★   ★   ★

Following the defeat of the Loyalists, Eddie returned to Los Angeles in 1940. By then Evangelist Carter and his wife were also in Los Angeles, having been forced to flee China because of the Japanese onslaught. By chance Eddie met his father on the street one day, but the two men had little to say to each other. Eddie steered clear of the old man and his wife. He was on his own now, supporting himself with odd jobs, and amusing himself with the vibrant night life to be found in the Central Avenue area.

Central Avenue was the heart of the rapidly growing Los Angeles black community. Day and night the streets were crowded with people, and for young men like Eddie there was no lack of exciting things to do. Jazz clubs like Club Alabam' were hotspots that throbbed with music and dancers every night. Lena Horne, Paul Robeson, and other top black performers entertained enthusiastic audiences at the Shriners Temple and other venues. Young NAACP activists met regularly at the YMCA at 28th and Central to organize a campaign for better parts for black actors in Hollywood films. Good food and good times could be found at Ella's Café and the many other thriving restaurants that lined the avenue.

It was on one of his outings that Eddie encountered and quickly fell in love with Mildred Hoover, the widowed daughter of a black family well known in the community. They met at a restaurant that was popular with young people. A strikingly beautiful woman, Mildred dressed stylishly and gave the impression of being a cultured

Mildred and Eddie Carter in Los Angeles, 1940.

young woman—which she was. She caught his eye right away. Eddie himself was very handsome with a youthful, debonair presence. Clean-cut and meticulous about his dress, he wasn't a tall man. He had a compact, athletic build, and he carried himself with the ease and confidence of someone who had seen much of the world. Using the charm that came easily to him, he introduced himself and they talked, each taken with the other. Mildred told him that her family ran a boardinghouse. Eddie said he was interested in finding a nice place to stay. She took him to see the boardinghouse and meet her parents.

Mildred's mother, Maycola, came from New Orleans, where Mildred was born. Mildred never knew her father. Her mother had married James Jennings shortly after arriving in Los Angeles. Her mother was a maid for a white judge, and Jennings worked for another white family. Hardworking and frugal, they saved their money and soon acquired the boardinghouse where Eddie met them.

Eddie was in awe of Mildred. Not only was she beautiful, but she was a cultured person—a violinist who as a girl played at major churches and was well known in the black middle-class community as a parlor room performer. She went on to become the first black violinist with the Los Angeles Philharmonic Orchestra. Eddie desired her, but she seemed unattainable to him. As he later wrote in a letter to her: "The first time I saw you, you scared the daylights out of me. You were what I wanted and didn't hope to get. . . . I was darn lucky to get you."

Attracted not only by Mildred but by the warm atmosphere he found at her parent's boardinghouse, a modest frame house on East 22nd Street, Eddie took a room. Mildred's family became his family. Eddie especially adored Mr. Jennings, a sweet, gentle man. He was the father Eddie felt he had never had.

William, Eddie's brother, was living in New York but soon joined the Army. Eddie's sister, Miriam, who was

also living in Los Angeles, moved into the boardinghouse
for a short time. Miriam worked at a drugstore and was
something of a naughty party girl. Once when Eddie
knocked on her door, she greeted him with "Hello fella.
What's it going to be, tricks or treats?" Eddie was annoyed
by what he considered her "wild" behavior. On the other
hand, Mildred, an only child used to being the queen bee,
enjoyed Miriam's boldness, and they became great
friends.

Mildred had married very young, but her husband, an
alcoholic, died of liver disease, leaving her with two small
children, Iris and Charles. Although she was a parent,
Mildred was also a young woman who enjoyed going out
and having fun with her friends. In fact, her parents had
once put her in a convent for a year to slow her down.
She introduced Eddie to her circle of friends as the two of
them began going out. So Eddie not only gained a girl-
friend, he acquired surrogate parents, children, and a
whole social world. Through Mildred's family and Mildred's friends he became intimately familiar for the first
time with the culture and aspirations of middle-class
African Americans. The stage was set and all he had to do
was show up.

It wasn't long before nature took its course and Mildred became pregnant. Edward III, nicknamed "Buddha"
for his rotund appearance and bald head, was born
March 27, 1941.

Meanwhile, as the fighting in Europe and Asia spread,

calls for U.S. intervention were increasing. Ever since Italy's invasion of Ethiopia in 1935, the black community had watched these developments with growing concern. Many black men were willing to heed the call to arms, but there was also a degree of skepticism. Black men had fought in World War I only to come home to renewed racism. For the black community, World War II would be regarded as a war on two fronts. Labor leader A. Philip Randolph, head of the Brotherhood of Sleeping Car Porters, the country's largest and most powerful black labor union, set the tone in January 1941, when he and other civil rights leaders called for a march on Washington to protest discrimination in the war industries and the armed forces.

Faced with the threat of 100,000 black people marching on Washington, in June 1941, President Franklin Roosevelt issued Executive Order 8802, ordering an end to racial discrimination in the defense industry. Although the armed forces remained segregated, Roosevelt's order represented an important step forward. The war itself would bring about more changes. In December 1941, Japanese fighter planes attacked the U.S. Navy fleet at Pearl Harbor. A Navy messman named Dorie Miller became the first black hero of the war when he seized an antiaircraft gun on the stricken USS *West Virginia* and single-handedly shot down four of the attacking Japanese planes. Early in 1942, as the United States launched a full-scale war mobilization, the *Pittsburgh Courier*, an influential black newspaper, gave symbolic expression to the feelings of black Americans when it proclaimed its immensely popular "Double V" campaign: victory over fascism abroad and victory over racism at home.

Eddie had decided to enlist in the Army well before the attack on Pearl Harbor. A veteran of the struggle against Japanese invaders in China and of the Spanish Civil War, he was acutely aware of the military threat presented by fascism. No doubt his familiarity with military life and his lack of a civilian career also contributed to his decision to enlist. He signed up on September 26, 1941. Shortly afterward, he found himself on a train headed for boot camp in Camp Wolters, Texas.

Eddie was shocked by the racial conditions he found in Texas. "Conditions down here are pretty bad," he wrote to Mildred on October 6. "I mean the South. The rotten South. Only the damned live here." He didn't give any details in the letter, but given his background and youth spent abroad, this was probably his first encounter with overt racial segregation and discrimination. In a letter on October 14 he mentioned that some of the other new recruits got into trouble and were jailed. Whether the trouble was due to racial incidents, youthful brawling, or problems with white officers was not made clear, but Eddie made it plain that he wanted to avoid trouble. "Everything I am told to do, I go ahead and do it for your sake," he wrote to Mildred. "It seems to make life a lot easier when I look at it that way. I would be a pretty tough guy down here if it were not for the thought of you. It goes to prove I think the world of you."

Significantly, Eddie always addressed his letters to "Mrs. Edward A. Carter Jr." and in his letters he often referred to Mildred as his wife and himself as her husband. They were not yet married, and in joining the Army Eddie wasn't running away from her. If anything, he wanted to do something to prove that he was worthy of her. Eddie sought always to keep his desire to be husband and wife before Mildred. Through his letters he continued his courtship. He wrote almost daily—sometimes twice a day—and in every letter he professed his ardor for her. In one letter he included a clipping from the First Platoon newsletter with an item reporting that "Private Edward A. Carter doesn't say much, he is so busy writing and receiving letters. Wonder if love could be the answer?????" He appended a handwritten comment: "It's the truth. See?" Eddie went so far as to get Edwin Kennedy, an Army friend of his, to write a note to Mildred avowing that "Your husband will not move from the barracks at all—all he does is write to you and talk of you." Kennedy included some pencil sketches of Eddie in uniform, marching, writing letters, and reading a letter to Mildred to which she responds "No." Eddie stopped at nothing to persuade Mildred of his love for her and his desire to marry her. When Mildred sent him a card, cigarettes, and other gifts at Christmas, Eddie responded with an eight-page letter expressing his gratitude. "You are my ideal," he gushed. "I am living only to be able to come back to your warm and beautiful love." Eddie did not fail to express his affection for the children and Mildred's family. "I am dying to see little Buddha," he wrote. In subsequent letters he asked about Buddha's development: Did he have any hair on his head yet? Had he taken a step or spoken a first word? Special greetings were often directed to Mr. Jennings, to whom Eddie felt very close. Eddie also included Mildred's two children by her previous marriage in his notion of their family, speaking of them as "my kids."

From the first day he entered boot camp Eddie baffled his instructors. They couldn't understand how a new recruit, after very little training, could achieve near perfect scores in shooting. "I don't miss a thing I shoot at," Eddie wrote to Mildred. Moreover, he was proficient with a host of weapons, including handguns, rifles, antitank weapons, and the Thompson submachine gun, his favorite. Proud of his accomplishment, Eddie sent Mildred an article published in the post newspaper in October praising his marksmanship. The article predicted that Private Carter "will become one of the area's, if not one of the camp's, best shots."

Training at the boot camp was intense, and shortly before it ended in early January a tragedy was narrowly averted. Eddie lost his footing on ice on a march and fell off a dam into a reservoir with an eighty-pound pack strapped to his back. He sank like a rock into the deep water. Unable to swim under all the weight, he stayed calm and managed to release the straps and buckles and free himself from the heavy pack. He struggled to the surface, much to the surprise of the officers and the other soldiers, who thought he would surely drown. They told him he had been under water for four minutes, but to him it seemed like four days. It was so cold that his clothes froze when he climbed out of the water. But with a cockiness that was characteristic of him, Eddie told Mildred not to worry. "I am fit as a fiddle," he boasted.

With his weapons skills, discipline, and can-do attitude, Eddie quickly gained the respect of the white officers. However, because of the Army's policy of racial segregation, Eddie and the other black soldiers were to be assigned to a service unit—as cooks, truck drivers, stevedores, engineers—rather than to combat duty.

After completing basic training Eddie was shipped out to Fort Benning, Georgia, and assigned to 3535th Quartermaster Truck Company. In less than a year he would be promoted to staff sergeant. But if Eddie was shocked by the racism he found in Texas, he was appalled by what he found in Georgia. Both the civilian white population and the Army were bastions of racism. "They don't treat you at all like soldiers," he complained. "It's more like slaves. When this war is over, you'll see plenty of tough and bitter boys coming home," he prophesied, with more truth than he could have known.

Two days later he voiced his anger, bitterness, and despair at the mistreatment of black people, especially black soldiers, by whites. In a letter to Mildred dated January 25, 1942, he wrote:

"After I get out of the Army and should [the United States] have another war, I'll not join the Army. I'll go to jail before I go. The treatment that they give the Negro in the South is plenty of reason. If that is what we have to fight for, why fight? Fight to save the white man's money? The Negro is nothing but the cat's paw. I have every bit of love and respect I ever had for the United States. I know I shouldn't be telling you these things. But why should the Negro fight for something he will not get? Should we fight for mops, buckets, and brooms, and then be treated as they are treating us? Hell no! We fight, then we should be able to break bread and eat it together with the rest of our white brothers. 'All men are created equal.' If so, why can't we share the spoils?

"The officers down here tell us that they don't need niggers in the Army. Then why in the hell don't they let us go. After all, a mop, bucket, and broom are not worth giving one's life for. The white man is the lowest animal there is. Nothing is too low or dirty for him to do." Sensing that his anger might worry Mildred, Eddie added, "I am letting my hate get the best of me. So please overlook my top blowing."

Eddie seemed to take a deep breath and then he continued his letter: "The main thing is that I still love you,

Mil. Nothing will ever stop me from coming home. . . . I dreamed of you last night, sweets. I dreamed that we were out boat riding on a beautiful lake. The water was clear as glass. Everything looked beautiful. Even as you do. Nothing will stop my being true."

In the steady flow of what he called his "epistles" to Mildred he insisted that he wanted her to come to him and get married. But there was some hesitation—on both sides. Eddie loved Mildred but he was afraid of getting too close to someone for fear of losing her, as he had lost his mother. Mildred stirred tender feelings in him and this had a strong impact on him, but he still had doubts that she would truly want him as her husband. She wasn't a needy person. She had a secure and full life. As for Mildred, she was captivated by Eddie, but having come through a difficult relationship with her former husband, she was worried about stability and commitment. She also sensed Eddie's hesitation, but she didn't know its source. With Eddie now a soldier and far away, she probably worried that they might drift apart, that he might not remain faithful to her.

Each of them struggled with doubts, but eventually they agreed that Mildred should come to Georgia and they would get married. Mildred joined him in May 1942, and they were married on June 10. Mildred left Iris and Charles with her parents in Los Angeles. Iris suffered with asthma, and Mildred was fearful that the humid Southern climate would affect her adversely. Eddie was worried that, given the hostile racial climate in the South, a rambunctious young black boy might fall in harm's way. The family settled in a small, cramped house in the nearby town of Columbus. Although their life was circumscribed, Eddie was happy to have Mildred and Buddha with him.

Despite his anger over Southern racism voiced in his letters to Mildred, Eddie was doing well in the Army and gaining some notoriety. In October 1942, he was featured in an article in *The Pine-Bur*, the post newspaper. The article noted that his "career as a soldier of fortune has taken him around the world." It recounted his growing up in India and China, and his combat experience in China and Spain. "He is now married and the proud father of a large son," the article ended.

A year after marrying Eddie, Mildred gave birth to a second son, William. They named William for Eddie's brother, who was in the service at a different military base. With Mildred, Eddie felt a wholeness he had never known before.

Meanwhile, his relationship with his own family had reached a nadir. Eddie and his brother William had always been close. William had been married for a short time, but his wife walked out on him, leaving him heartbroken. Eddie's relationship with Miriam, whom he regarded as out of control, was often strained. And since returning to the United States, Eddie had kept his distance from his father and stepmother. He wrote to them occasionally but complained that they didn't respond. "They don't answer my letters," Eddie told Mildred, "so I'll discontinue my letters." The old wound between father and son never healed, and now it had become an ugly scar.

CHAPTER FIVE

LOVE AND WAR: A HERO'S STORY

E ddie loved married life and he greatly enjoyed his young family. Despite the evident segregation and discrimination, he also relished his life in the Army. His officers were impressed by his knowledge, capability, and enthusiasm, and as a result he was promoted to staff sergeant. But Eddie was a combat soldier, a warrior against tyranny, and he was itching to get into the fight against fascism.

In the fall of 1944 his hopes were raised when his unit was notified that they would be shipped overseas. He packed up his family and sent them back to Mildred's parents in Los Angeles. His truck company was shipped first to England and then on November 13, 1944, they arrived in southern France expecting to be sent to the front lines. Instead they were assigned to transporting supplies to the fighting forces and cleaning out snipers in the rear areas.

Despite his disappointment, Eddie kept an upbeat tone in his letters home. On November 22 he wrote to Mildred to wish her a happy birthday. "Dear Pet: You see,

I haven't forgotten the date. Dec. 1st is your birthday, is it not? If I wasn't several thousand miles away I would give you one thousand burning kisses for your very own. This is another one of my letters you may keep as a promissory note to be made good at the first opportunity. In the meanwhile, I'll be thinking only of you. If you should care to make me happy, write soon and mail me a few crumbs of that birthday cake, which I'm sure your mother baked for the sweetest of girls."

In a letter written on December 17, Eddie admitted the deep impact Mildred's love had made in his life: "Your claim is that you do not understand me—yet you are the only one who has ever understood me. You made me love you when once upon a time I was sure that it was impossible for me to love anyone but my mother. You did what others could not do. You are my emancipator. Life would be unbearable without having someone to fight for and to come home to after the war." For most of his life Eddie had steeled himself against feelings of tenderness for anyone other than his mother. Mildred taught him to love again.

Eddie was a soldier and he was anxious to get into the infantry. From the moment he landed in Europe he volunteered daily for combat duty. He wanted to get to the front lines, but he was never accepted. Finally he got his chance. The German counteroffensive at Ardennes, the Battle of the Bulge, took a disastrous toll. Reinforcements were desperately needed, but few GIs—that is, few white

GIs—were available. Thousands of black troops stood at the ready, and many of them were eager to join combat units. Having no alternative, the Army finally opened its ranks to black volunteers. An initial circular soliciting volunteers stated that black soldiers would be assigned to units without regard to race or color and implied that they would be fighting side by side with white troops. This was hastily retracted and replaced by a new circular stating that volunteers would be accepted with-out regard to race or color, with no suggestion of inter-racial fighting units. In fact, the black volunteers would be assigned to all-black infantry units under the com-mand of white officers, in accordance with the policy adopted by General Eisenhower and the Army. The all-black units would operate within the structure of larger white units.

Some 4,500 black soldiers volunteered; 2,800 were accepted for training, and 2,221 made it into combat duty. Sergeant Carter was among the first to be accepted, but like other black sergeants, he was required to relinquish his stripes and accept a reduction in rank to private. The Army didn't want any black sergeants supervising white enlisted men. Eddie had worked hard to earn the rank of sergeant, but he gladly gave it up to serve his country on the front lines.

Eddie continued to write frequently to Mildred. The Army prohibited soldiers from disclosing details of their whereabouts or combat operations, but Eddie kept her apprised of his well-being. In addition to inquiring about her and the children, he could turn on the charm when he wanted to and his letters often waxed romantic. Eddie professed his everlasting love for Mildred, although at the same time he admitted harboring some misgivings about emotional expressiveness.

Jan. 3rd 1945
France

Dear Lover,

I have always found . . . that the time I spend writing to you to be my holy and sacred hour of the day. The time that I spend in writing to you, my sweets, is the only time that I ever make a confession. And it seems to me that I'll always be guilty of the same sin. Or is it a sin? Well, it seems that I'm guilty of Loving You. Please do not condemn me, because I shall only continue to confess my Love and devotion to you alone. . . . Married life I have found to be one of the sweetest of all experiences. Life was tragic until my lucky star, You, came into this life of mine. For Love's sake alone, I promise you there will never be, let's see, I guess you might call it the state of stagnation for us. Again I promise, as I have in my other letters, to reimburse you for every lonely second, hour, day, week, month, and year that I have been forced to spend away from your charms and that radiant, tender, consuming Love that you alone possess and have given to me so freely. Is my confession complete, sweetheart? I am trying to confess that which is in this heart of mine. My way of expression I admit is crude, but please try and comprehend. What I have written comes from the heart and not from reasoning. If I were to follow the code that I have always tried to live by, I would never admit my Love and feelings for any woman, not even to myself. Because I have always felt, that is until meeting you, that to express one's Love and devotion could only mean that the person or persons were weak. And I the one who has lived by these same codes have broken them. "I was blind and now I see!" Now I am quoting the Bible and that's not at all like myself. If there is anything that I have failed to admit or own up to, please let me know. (Amen)

Kiss the children by proxy for me. Give my Love and good wishes to the family....

As for myself, I am still in the very best of health and will continue to make the best of a bad situation. The harder I work and fight to draw this war to a speedy close, the sooner my return.... Sweets, I must sound retreat until another day of light. Loads of Love, all of my Love. Thumbs up. Write whenever your time permits.

For Ever and Ever,
Eddie (Amen)

P. S. I still Love You only.

In January 1945, as a bitterly cold winter gripped Europe, Eddie was assigned to the Ground Force Reinforcement Command in France to be trained with other black volunteers as combat soldiers. At the completion of the training period Eddie was assigned to the Twelfth Armored Division, Fifty-sixth Armored Infantry Battalion, Provisional Company 1 (also known as D Company, or Dog Company). The commanding officer of D Company was First Lieutenant Floyd Vanderhoef; Lieutenant Russell Blair was the executive officer. At the time of his new assignment on March 12, 1945, Eddie had no idea that he was about to take part in one of the largest assaults in the history of the war, the Rhineland assault, under the leadership of General George Patton. The Twelfth Armored Division had been temporarily assigned from the Seventh Army to Patton's Third Army, where it would become known as Patton's famous "Mystery Division." The orders for the change came down on March 17. The Twelfth Armored was ordered to move from Saint Avold to an area near Siereck Les Baines, where it was attached to the Third Army's XX Corps. The Mystery Division came into being as shoulder patches and unit vehicle markings were removed. The Hellcats, as Twelfth Armored members proudly called their unit, were now part of Patton's "Blood and Guts" Third Army.

The Third Army had been given the task of crossing the Rhine River. Patton was anxious to beat the British, who were under the command of Field Marshal Bernard

Montgomery. He was determined that his troops would be the first to make a successful assault across the river. Under tight security the Twelfth Armored moved into a position near Trier, Germany, from which it could spear-head the drive to the Rhine. The plan was to pass through the Ninety-fourth Infantry Division, race to the river, and secure a crossing. Mopping up enemy strongholds would be the job of the infantry unit that followed in the wake of the assault.

"As we advanced toward Trier," Dog Company's Russell Blair remembered, "we were pretty exposed, riding on top of tanks and in wide-open six-by-six trucks in an armored column. Whenever we encountered any action, the troops would deploy in front of and to the side of the tanks, with the tanks firing over their heads. Carter was doing a good job with his squad, and the men respected him."

Company commander Vanderhoef was also impressed by Eddie. "Blair and I were trying to develop leaders for the squads. We promoted several of the black soldiers. Carter was the first one. He was the ideal soldier. He wanted to do the right thing. He had absolutely no qualms about being there, and he insisted that his men do what they were supposed to do. He was one of the best leaders we had in that company."

The Twelfth Armored Division was organized into three combat commands, each consisting of tanks, armored infantry, and artillery. Eddie's unit, the Fifty-sixth Infantry, was made part of Combat Command B (CCB). The units advanced into Germany and across the Saar Palatinate, making steady headway and taking hundreds of Germans prisoner. Smashed German equipment littered the route. The orders were to keep going and search for an intact bridge at the town of Ludwigshafen. The units met strong resistance at Freimheim, but this did not stop the advance. CCB pushed on and cut the autobahn, a segment of German's vaunted superhighway system. In the advance from Birkenfeld to Ramsen on March 20, some 2,200 German soldiers were taken prisoner and another 1,000 enemy troops killed. Late that night elements of the Fifty-sixth infantry reached the Rhine River.

The Germans had blown up the bridge at Ludwigshafen so the Americans bivouacked at a little town nearby. The next day, March 22, CCB was sent along the Rhine to attack Speyer and capture the bridge across the Rhine there. "We knew from reconnaissance," Blair said, "that there were some thick woods between Ludwigshafen and Speyer, with a heavy German force. Late in the afternoon they moved Dog Company into position to clean out the woods the next day so that we wouldn't have a problem when we attacked Speyer." Blair was assigned to take the command vehicles and bivouac in what had formerly been an SS barracks. "The next morning, March 23, the weather was beautiful. At daylight D Company jumped off to clean the woods out, but the Germans had withdrawn during the night. They pulled D Company back to join the attack on Speyer."

As Eddie and his rifle squad were riding on a tank advancing toward the town, the column came under bazooka and small-arms fire from a large warehouse. Everyone scattered and took cover. Quickly surveying the situation, Eddie volunteered to lead three men to reconnoiter the warehouse. Two of his men were killed and the third wounded within minutes. Eddie advanced alone, despite being wounded himself multiple times, managing to silence two machine-gun nests and a mortar crew. Within thirty yards of the warehouse he took cover behind an earthen bank.

His own officers thought he was probably dead and commenced shooting at the warehouse with a rocket launcher. Eddie waited there for two hours when a squad of German soldiers, checking to see if he was dead, approached his position. Waiting until the right moment, he leapt up and opened fire with his Thompson submachine gun. He cut down six of the Germans, and the other two quickly surrendered. Using the two prisoners as a shield, one in front of him and the other behind, Eddie made his way back across the field to his unit.

Vanderhoef and Blair were amazed to see Eddie return with the two prisoners. Even though he was wounded, he refused to be evacuated to a hospital until be had climbed to an observation post established by the officers and pointed out German machine-gun positions.

With this help and the information obtained from the prisoners Eddie captured, the American forces cleared the road and continued their advance into Speyer. Eddie, though wounded and alone, had defeated a last-ditch German effort to stop the American advance.

The bridge at Speyer was blown up by the retreating Germans, but American tanks were ferried across the Rhine and soon engineers built a treadway bridge across the river at Nierstein. The Rhineland drive by Patton's Mystery Division was unstoppable.

While recovering from his wounds in an Army hospital, Eddie wrote to Mildred to tell her of his condition: "Dear Lover: Just a line or two letting you know that I am still able to kick. Sweets, please overlook my not writing sooner. We have been fighting pretty steady. I have killed and killed Jerries until I couldn't see straight. I guess the War Dept. has written you concerning my getting shot up a little. A Jerry machine gun hit me in my left hand— three holes in my left arm, one hole in my left leg, two holes in my right leg and one hole in the right foot. And also in the head. I have nine bullet holes in all. Not so bad at that, is it? I hope that I'll get well in time so that I can get back to my outfit. I would sure like to get to Berlin. My outfit has the fightingest bunch of doughboys there is in it." In the hospital Eddie was presented with a Purple Heart, which he promptly sent to Mildred for safekeeping. By then he had also earned two Battle Stars.

Eddie followed with more of his usual chatty, upbeat letters: "How is everything with exotic you?" he wrote in another. "As for myself, well, I have never felt better. By the time you get this letter I should be on my way to Berlin. I have a score to settle with Jerry. Although I was shot up a bit, I feel as though I can outfight any Jerry on two feet. We of the armored infantry are the first to make the break through in the Jerry lines. And then the regular infantry follows after us. So you see, we go through a lot of hell. Only Jerry catches one hell of a lot more. The American doughboy is one darn good soldier. General Patton, as you already know, is our leader. One thing I like about him is that he has plenty of guts. He is a regular G.I. Joe."

When weeks passed and he didn't get a letter from Mildred—the Army's mail system was understandably erratic in the middle of a war—Eddie wrote longingly: "I haven't heard from you for so long that I am only able to picture you as a dream. Sometimes I wonder if I have ever been in the USA. Just like India and China—all are dreams."

When Eddie was wounded, the War Department sent a telegram to Mildred advising that her husband was "slightly wounded" in Germany and that she could continue to send mail to him as before. Mildred sent back an anxious telegram to Eddie asking him to write immediately and telling him that she had written every day. Almost none of Mildred's letters to Eddie survived the war. One letter that did survive was written on April 10,

1945. Mildred voiced her anxiety about his love for her and her feelings of helplessness.

Darling Eddie,

I am very tired tonight but I thought I'd try to stay awake long enough to pen you more lines. Tonight I've been wondering what your thoughts of me are, if any? Do you ever really think of me? Do I stay with you as you seem to stay with me? Are you sure you still love me? I couldn't stand it if you didn't. Darling, I am still as proud as ever of the sweetest little soldier in all the world to me. My heart is breaking because there is absolutely nothing that I can do for you when you need me most. I should be with you to consolate [*sic*] you when the going gets tough. Darling, please forgive my helplessness. My hands are tied by many miles. God, if this war would only end and let you come home again. I promise you my life will be dedicated to one cause. Making you happy, comfortable and loved. Darling, I shall try to make up to you all of the horrible things that have come your way. I shall love you until you forget this hellish war. Keep your chin up. Get well.

Love, Mil

P.S. All of my love belongs to you only. You are still my heart's desire. I still thrill at your memory, Darling. It shall never die. Get well soon. I love you Eddie.

Impatient to get back to the action, after a month Eddie slipped out of the Army hospital and made his way back to the front lines. Russell Blair, by then promoted to captain, recalled this unexpected development:

"I didn't see Carter again until later in April. We were close to Bad Tolz down below Munich. By this time the German resistance was pretty much shattered, and some days we could move along at forty or fifty miles a day. One day Carter showed up back at the company. I was surprised to see him; wounded soldiers don't ordinarily get well that quick. I asked how'd he got back. He said he was released from the hospital in Luxembourg by his doctors. He looked fine. He didn't show any signs of having been wounded. We were glad to have him back, but a short time later we got a message from the hospital saying that he was AWOL. We wired back to the hospital that he was back on active duty at the front, and we didn't hear any more about that. We had a good laugh about it.

"I came to find out in talking with Carter that he had met a captain out of the Tenth Armored Division who was also at the hospital. The captain was getting released and returning to the Tenth Armored, which was located near us. Carter decided he was ready to return to duty, so he just caught a ride in the captain's jeep and got dropped off at our rear. Eddie Carter was one phenomenal soldier."

After returning to his unit, Eddie fought with the Fifty-sixth Armored Infantry Battalion through the last mopping-up operations of the war. In combat the two white officers of Eddie's platoon were wounded and he was made acting platoon sergeant. Meanwhile, the officers of D Company considered making a recommendation that Sergeant Carter be awarded a decoration for his bravery at Speyer. While there was no doubt that he deserved a medal, there was a feeling that, given the attitude in the Army, if he were recommended for a Medal of Honor he wouldn't get it. Some thought he would have a better chance of winning a Distinguished Service Cross.

While the officers mulled over their decision, the men in Carter's unit welcomed him back as a hero, a tough guy whom the Germans couldn't kill. But Eddie was focused as much on love as he was on war. In a letter on his birthday, May 26, he wrote that "after getting shot up and coming back to my same outfit everyone seems to think that I am a hero. I have told the boys that I am a hero to only one person, my wife." He went on to tell her that the men kidded him "about not getting myself a woman," and he claimed he sent one soldier to the hospital for suggesting that the 4-Fs (the civilian men at home exempted from military service) were "taking care of" Mildred. But decking the messenger couldn't banish the thought. Eddie ended with an appeal to Mildred that revealed his worry: "Remember that I am true to you only. I want to love you only. I can wait until I get back. Please try and wait for me."

In the closing days of the war D Company arrived outside a river town near the Alps. Meeting no resistance,

Eddie's platoon advanced into the town and took control of a German hospital. The war seemed about over. The next day the company moved to the river to protect a bridge—and were shocked to discover that the Germans were not yet finished. Out of the blue a German Messerschmitt fighter plane suddenly came barreling over the bridge late in the afternoon. Men scattered and ran for cover, but antiaircraft gunners quickly drew a bead on the German intruder and brought the fighter plane down with a burst of fire. The pilot bailed out and was captured. This dramatic encounter was the Fifty-sixth Armored Infantry Battalion's last combat action of the war.

For the next few months D Company found itself shifted around Germany as part of what was now an army of occupation. It was charged with guarding German prisoners of war and captured ammunition dumps. Robert Cabbell, another member of the Fifty-sixth Armored Infantry Battalion, remembered that there were also lighter moments during this period. Cabbell said Captain Blair organized a company softball team, and the team even challenged the white divisional all-stars to a game.

In June, Eddie happily wrote Mildred that he had just learned his name was "way! way! way! up on top of the list" of men soon to be discharged from the Army. He said when he got home Mildred must stop working and he would take her on a two- or three-week honeymoon. But even as he wrote of coming home, Eddie had a momentary thought about staying in the Army. He dismissed it as a long shot. "I think enough of you and the kids to want to come home," he said. "I must come home!"

Dog Company was deactivated in late July near Wallerstein, Germany. One of Captain Blair's last acts was to sign a recommendation for a Distinguished Service Cross for Sergeant Carter. Carter certainly deserved it, Blair remembered, for his bravery at Speyer and more. "He was one of the best soldiers I've ever seen," Blair said. Blair was then sent to testify as a character witness in a military trial. By the time he returned to Wallerstein, D Company had been broken up and its members were on the way to other duty or to Le Havre for the return home. But the men of D Company did not depart without sending a final message to battalion headquarters expressing their appreciation to Vanderhoef and Blair:

> We, the members of Dog Company, have found it to be a great pleasure and honor to serve and fight as part of the Fifty-sixth Battalion.
> Since joining the Battalion on 6 March under the command of Captain Vanderhoef and later under Captain Russell T. Blair, we can say that we were never treated more royally. Now that we are about to leave the Battalion, all of us would like to convey our sincere appreciation to Battalion Headquarters Staff

Sergeant Carter at the end of World War II
in 1945 in Wallerstein, Germany.

and all the Companies of the Fifty-sixth for the swell treatment you all gave us.

We wish all of you the best of luck in the world— and thanks for everything until we meet again.

The Doughs of Dog Company

Blair returned to the United States to go to flight school and become an Army Air Force pilot. He served as a combat pilot in Korea and retired in 1957 as a lieutenant colonel. Vanderhoef also stayed in the Army and served in Korea; he retired as a lieutenant colonel in 1961.

The black combat volunteers had served honorably and well. In the final weeks of the war, General Benjamin O. Davis toured the field and found that, despite limited training and experience, the black volunteers' courage in battle gained them the respect of white troops and commanders. Complaints mainly had to do with lack of training for certain assignments, he found. In spite of the praise, as Ulysses Lee points out in *The Employment of Negro Troops,* in some units "there arose an undercurrent of misgivings about retaining these troops within units once the war was over and battalions and regiments settled into occupation and garrison duties."

Many black combat veterans with relatively low combat duty points were reassigned to the old segregated service as stevedores, truck drivers, cooks, and engineers. Others, like Sergeant Carter, with high combat duty points were assigned to the Sixty-ninth Infantry Division for return to the United States.

For some of the black soldiers in the Fifty-sixth Armored Infantry Battalion, including Sergeant Carter, the return home would be traumatic in itself. Robert Hale, another volunteer in the Fifty-sixth, remembered being harassed by white soldiers as he and others in his unit attempted to board ship.

"We were at Cherbourg, France, about to get onto boxcars to ride to the port when we had a problem with some white guys in the Thirty-sixth Infantry Division. Some platoon sergeant brought his platoon down and mounted up his machine guns and started calling us every name he could think of. Some of our guys wanted to fight, but cooler heads prevailed, saying you can't fight machine guns with pistols or knives. Fortunately, our division commander came down and saw what was happening. He got the division commander of the Thirty-sixth to intervene. The Thirty-sixth commander said the sergeant was taking unauthorized action and reduced that sergeant to a private right there. It was sort of disheartening. As long as we were up on the front line with them we were buddies, but as soon as the war ended they became our enemies again."

Things were not necessarily any better for black soldiers after returning to the United States. Evanda Kiel, who also saw combat in the Fifty-sixth Infantry, remembered being discharged from Fort McPherson in Georgia after the war.

"I was about to go into the bus station in Atlanta to buy a ticket to go home. I was greeted at the front door by the military police and the civilian police. They shook their nightsticks at me and said, 'You can't come through here, boy.' I was wearing my uniform and my combat infantryman's badge, so they knew I was a soldier returning from the war. I was proud of having served in the Army, but then I came back to this. That really broke my heart. I could have been killed for my country during the war, and I came back and couldn't walk through the front door of a public bus station. That was a disgrace."

Eddie, too, would encounter problems as a black veteran returning home. He would discover that he was targeted for a special kind of trouble.

CHAPTER SIX

UNDER SURVEILLANCE

Following an honorable discharge from the Army on September 30, 1945, Eddie was welcomed to Los Angeles as a returning hero. In November, the Army announced that he had received the Distinguished Service Cross, and the story was widely circulated in the press. The next month he was invited to be an honored guest and recipient of an award at a Welcome Home, Joe dinner sponsored by American Youth for Democracy. Unknown to him, as I discovered in my research at the National Archives, this group was under surveillance by military intelligence as a suspected Communist Party organization. Others to receive awards at the dinner for their "contributions to American citizenship and democracy" included singer Frank Sinatra and syndicated cartoonist Bill Mauldin, as well as other veterans. Military intelligence thought it worth noting that one of the "embittered" veterans—who was not named in the report—attending the dinner denounced "the so-called democracy for which they fought" only to return "to find

America more prejudiced than before and intolerance at an all-time high."

The Welcome Home, Joe affair prompted a reporter to write a feature story about Eddie. The story appeared in the *Daily World*, a Communist Party newspaper published in California. As I surmised from the newspaper clippings I found in Mildred's trunk, Eddie apparently never turned down a request for an interview, whether it was for the post newspaper at an Army base or an African-American magazine or a Communist Party newspaper.

Authored by Fred Vast and published December 13, 1945, the *Daily World* article gave an account of the battle at Speyer, as well as Eddie's experiences in Europe and since returning home. The piece included a photograph of Sergeant Carter in uniform wearing his decorations and a caption announcing that the "Negro hero" was honored at a Welcome Home, Joe dinner. Vast's account suggested that Sergeant Carter was awarded a DSC instead of a Medal of Honor because of racial discrimination. Asserting that Carter was told by the officers that he would be recommended for the Medal of Honor, Vast then pointed out that "Carter is a Negro and not one Negro received the top medal."

According to the article, racial mistreatment figured prominently in Sergeant Carter's experiences. Eddie was quoted on the military's refusal to protect black soldiers stationed in Georgia for training. I knew from his letters that Eddie was angered by the racism he encountered there. "Yet there was nothing we could do," he told Vast. "There were no facilities for Negroes, so we walked the streets. For doing that we were always being attacked by white civilians and police. There were many beatings, jailings, and killings. Some of the boys were sent to the chain gangs for thirty to ninety days even though they hadn't done a thing. When they got out, the Army would court-martial them." This was graphic corroboration of the accounts in letters Eddie had written to Mildred about the racial situation in Georgia.

As for his experience in Europe, "it was just the opposite," he told the reporter. Despite hate stories spread by some white troops, European civilians, even Germans, were friendly and treated black American soldiers as fellow human beings.

Even some of the Southern white soldiers seemed to change their attitude in Europe. Some white troops told Eddie, "We didn't know how good you guys are. When we get home we're going to tell the people all about you." But as he was leaving Europe at the end of the war there was trouble, Eddie recounted, when white soldiers tried to stop black troops from boarding the ship to which they were assigned. Eddie's story echoed Robert Hale's account of the hostility directed against black troops departing from Cherbourg.

Looking back on his wartime experience Sergeant Carter told the reporter: "We fought for the recognition of our people, and we found democracy in the front lines. We fought because Hitler was the worst of two wrongs— worse than racial discrimination at home. We liberated Europe, but here at home we are not free. I just want a chance to earn a living, and I want to help finish the fight for freedom."

Welcome Home dinners aside, transitioning to civilian life was proving to be difficult. Eddie was happy to be back with his family, but it was not easy to find work. He finally landed a job as a cook in a private home in Beverly Hills. He also tried to get a loan from the Veterans Administration to set up a small paint-spraying business, but he had no success. Hopes dashed, he planned to save enough money to buy the equipment he needed for the business.

Eddie was not alone in experiencing problems in the transition to civilian life. Discrimination was widespread and many black veterans were having trouble finding work. An *Ebony* magazine article entitled "Where Are the Heroes?"—about black military men who won recognition during World War II—noted that "most [of the black heroes] have drifted into the obscurity of small towns, army hospitals and schools." The article continued: "Some are finding disillusionment in the discovery that medals are meaningless on a job hunt but most are acquainted with the hard facts of life in the U.S.A. and

*Eddie showing his World War II medals to sons Edward III ("Buddha")
and William ("Redd").*

pitching in to do their bit for a better tomorrow." Eddie told the *Ebony* reporter that while some gains had been made for blacks during the war, there was still much room for improvement—"about 99 per cent."

Having grown up outside the United States and having served in two armies before joining the U.S. Army, Eddie was unaccustomed to antiblack racial discrimination. He never got used to it. It angered him, and he found it difficult to conceal his anger. He could not adapt to a system whose racial etiquette demanded that black men bow and scrape before white people and then grin and bear it. A man of enormous self-discipline, he would bear it for the sake of his family, but he would not grin, he would not bow and scrape. In civilian life he discovered that he was just another anonymous Negro male. Despite its problems, in the Army, with its insistence on discipline and performance, he found a more congenial environment, one in which he might gain recognition.

Although Eddie was ambivalent about civilian life, he decided to give it a try. But he was not cut out for domestic service as a cook. He tried his hand at business, purchasing a surplus military landing craft for $200 and using its attention-getting quality to advertise local movies. Whimsically named the *Ruptured Duck*, the odd vehicle served for a time to take people out on fishing trips. Eddie, however, was not the kind of person to easily slap people on the back and keep them entertained with fishing stories. His days as a businessman were numbered, although

Eddie and Mildred with their sons, Redd and Buddha, in Los Angeles,
1946. In the background is the Army surplus amphibious landing vehicle
Eddie hoped to turn into a business.

he remained in business long enough to become briefly an
officer of the troubled Eastside Chamber of Commerce.

The chamber of commerce was established in 1937
with the purpose of advancing commercial, cultural, and
civic interests in the east section of the city. The organization also fought actively against racial discrimination in
employment. Composed mainly of local black businessmen and a handful of whites, the chamber of commerce
boasted a membership of two hundred by 1944. I knew
from my research that the FBI took an active interest in the

organization that year. In fact, in its November 1944 report on so-called foreign-inspired agitation among blacks in Los Angeles, the FBI devoted considerable attention to the doings of the Eastside Chamber of Commerce. On at least two occasions FBI informants, identified only as T-7 and T-8, reported on the chamber of commerce's activities.

According to the FBI report, on October 20, 1944, informant T-7 advised the FBI that the Eastside Chamber of Commerce was vitally interested in improving health conditions in the black community, especially with regard to venereal diseases. Apparently, military authorities were disturbed by an "alarming increase" of venereal disease among servicemen. Concluding that the "breakfast clubs," which operated during the hours from midnight to 8 A.M., were the main cause of the spread of venereal infection, the military had placed a number of these clubs off limits to military personnel.

This move by the military provoked a howl of protest from local tavern owners and civic leaders, especially when it became known that the military was considering placing the entire Central Avenue area, a thriving black business district, out of bounds. Meetings between community leaders and the military were hastily arranged. It was brought to the military's attention that such a change in policy might lead to black servicemen seeking recreation in white areas of the city, which, as the FBI report observed, would likely lead to racial unrest. The timely intervention of the Eastside Chamber of Commerce, in collaboration with military and naval authorities, produced a solution. Of course, any solution had to be in accord with the military's belief that it was best to keep black soldiers "within their element." After some discussion, the military and the businessmen agreed to a set of guidelines for bar and tavern owners to follow with regard to serving military personnel. Printed in the form of a circular, the plan was distributed to business owners in the Central Avenue area, to the apparent satisfaction of all concerned.

The FBI report shed light on the uneasy relationship between the military and the black community, but informant T-7 had a more direct interest in the Eastside Chamber of Commerce: sniffing out potential radicals in the organization. The chamber of commerce's policy was to accept businessmen as members regardless of their personal political beliefs, so long as they had no criminal record and did nothing to cause problems for the community or the "colored race" as a whole. This apparently left the door open for radicals to slip in, people whom T-7 referred to as "striped"—"radicals whom some people might consider as Communists." These members, however, kept their activity on such a plane as to not reflect on the chamber of commerce or the community as a whole and were therefore allowed to maintain their membership. The names of these "striped" members were not given in this summary report, though presumably T-7 passed them along to the FBI. There was no explanation of what they might have said or done that led T-7 to label them in such a way. Nor was there any suggestion that the FBI questioned T-7's characterization of these individuals. Apparently T-7's word alone was good enough for the FBI.

Informant T-8 was charged with the more mundane task of gathering statistical information, such as membership (200), annual dues ($12), and budget ($15,000, financed through subscription pledges).

Whether T-7 and T-8, or their equivalents, were still spying on the Eastside Chamber of Commerce in 1946, when Eddie was a member, is something I do not know. I found no records in my research to suggest that the chamber of commerce was under surveillance at that time, but given the FBI's intense interest in the threat of "racial unrest," it would seem likely that the agency was still keeping watch. By May 1946, Eddie was the chamber of commerce's director of public relations. Apparently, trouble of a financial nature had developed in the organization and an investigating committee was appointed to look into it. Two of the officers were queried and, according to accounts I found in the *Official East Side News*, refused to turn over records of bank balances and other information. The two officers were suspended by the executive committee in a meeting that Eddie was reported as attending.

Eddie and another board member were named to occupy the two ousted men's positions while the books were being checked. At the same time, it was announced that Sergeant Carter had agreed to become chairman of the Veterans Bureau of the organization. Eddie was highly regarded in the chamber of commerce. After all, he was a hero of many European campaigns and winner of the Distinguished Service Cross. According to the announcement, Sergeant Carter's first move would be to build a strong interracial veterans committee and to stage a big fund-raising supper to help build the committee. Perhaps Eddie's experiences in the war made him feel that black and white veterans might be able to work together and set an example for improving relations between the races.

He didn't get very far with his plans. His business ventures were not going well and he was worried about how he could support his family. With millions of white veterans returning from the war, black workers were pushed out of the skilled jobs they had gained as a result of President Roosevelt's desegregation of the defense plants. I'm sure Eddie did not relish the thought of seeking work as a common laborer or household servant.

At the same time, racial assaults on black people had increased after the war. For example, a huge battle was taking place in Los Angeles and throughout California over racially restrictive housing covenants that sought to prevent black families from buying homes in white neighborhoods. Black families that dared to challenge the covenants by moving into white neighborhoods were met with cross burnings, and other acts of intimidation. The black community was fighting back with lawsuits, protests, and various mobilizations—and in 1948 the California Supreme Court would finally outlaw restrictive covenants. It was a tense time as black veterans and civilians fought back against racist attacks. Government informants were busily looking for "subversives" in community organizations all over the place. Although I couldn't prove it, I had a strong feeling that Eddie's involvement in promoting an interracial veterans committee would have been viewed as suspicious by the authorities.

While Eddie may have seen in his interracial veterans committee a way to help the struggle against discrimination and mistreatment, his pressing need was for income to support his family. Once again, in the Army he would see a way to support his family in a manner that he felt was dignified and honorable. While the medals he had won meant little in civilian life, in the Army they were badges of recognition. In September 1946, he reenlisted, and by mid-October he was stationed at Camp Lee, Virginia, assigned as a staff sergeant to the First Group's Special Service. It didn't take him long to come to the attention of the camp newspaper. An article about his exploits in the war appeared on October 30 in the *Lee Traveller*. The article was completely laudatory and gave no hint of gathering clouds.

As he had done during his previous tour of duty, Eddie wrote faithfully to Mildred. By the end of October he was writing about plans for Mildred and the children to come to Virginia. He had investigated and found apartments suitable for the family. The weather was agreeable, and the cost of living was low. "We can live a darn sight cheaper than we could ever live in California," he wrote on October 28. "Virginia," he told Mildred, "is 90 percent better than Georgia. You haven't anything to fear."

Eddie had good reason for thinking so positively about his new life at Camp Lee. As a winner of the Distinguished Service Cross, he was held in high regard as a war hero. His experience and skills as a combat veteran were valued. At Camp Lee, Eddie hoped to find the success that had eluded him in Los Angeles. "The officers seem to think that I am an expert soldier. So I might as well stay where I am well thought of. I can make good here."

He promised to send Mildred some money to help her with the move to Virginia. The plan was for her to come there around January 10, after Eddie had arranged for a temporary apartment. Eddie said that the commanding general had promised to make available a three-bedroom apartment on the post in the late spring of 1947 as their permanent home. Eddie was overjoyed.

But instead, Eddie found himself on a train headed to California. The Army had other plans for him. Eddie was right in thinking that he was highly regarded by his immediate superiors. Those who worked directly with him always held him in high regard and considered him an outstanding soldier.

After the war the government made plans to reorganize state-level National Guards as federally recognized National Guard units capable of serving as trained reserves for the regular Army. In the view of military planners, the experience of World War II underscored the need for highly trained reserves that could be rapidly deployed in case of total war. Planners noted that the key to meeting this critical need was to select an elite group of expert soldiers from the regular Army to be detailed as instructors of the citizen-soldiers in state National Guard units, whose readiness for active duty would be certified by a federal recognition board. Because of his previous experience and outstanding war record, Eddie was hand-picked by his officers at Camp Lee to join this elite group of instructors.

But a national controversy erupted over the plans of some states, including Connecticut and California, to form new racially segregated National Guard units. Civil rights groups, especially local branches of the NAACP, strongly objected. California state officials responded that segregation was necessary to conform with Army racial policy. At its annual convention in 1947, the NAACP urged the secretary of war to order the integration of National Guard units.

War Department officials replied that the Army had no objections to integration; it was left up to each state to decide racial policy for Guard units. This was a rather disingenuous statement, since the Army was on record as opposing federal legislation to end racial segregation in the armed forces. Moreover, despite objections from the NAACP, the Army at the end of the war had routinely detached black combat volunteers from the white units in which they served and reassigned them to segregated service units. Nevertheless, the controversy, which was widely reported in the press, prompted the governor of Connecticut to voice his opposition to segregated Guard units. In California, on the other hand, there was no report of intervention by Governor Earl Warren. The state's adjutant general went ahead with plans to form headquarters companies of two battalions of an all-black Sixth Engineer Combat Group of the California National Guard.

Sergeant Carter reported to the adjutant general's office in Sacramento, where he met Sergeant Major Woodfred Jordan, the feisty veteran whom I later encountered at the Medal of Honor ceremony. Woodfred, another Army veteran, was also assigned to train guardsmen. The two were then posted to the National Guard Armory on Exposition Boulevard in the center of black Los Angeles, where the headquarters for the Sixth Engineer Combat Group was to be set up. At the armory, Sergeant Carter met and befriended other black soldiers, including Master

Sergeant Carter (holding weapon) training young National Guardsmen in California in 1947.

Sergeant Rance Richardson and Sergeant John Pulliams, who were assigned to the Guard.

From Los Angeles, Sergeant Carter was assigned to work as an instructor and adviser to the 1402d Engineer Combat Battalion at San Bernardino, under the command of Captain Frank W. Cleveland, a black veteran and respected community leader in Los Angeles.

By the summer of 1947, Sergeant Carter was at Camp Roberts in the mountains near San Luis Obispo giving the men their annual two weeks of intensive combat training. He also trained them in handling heavy equipment. Eddie was a regular presence at the weekly National Guard meetings during the rest of the year as well.

Eddie's assignment was both ironic and exciting. The irony was that during the war Eddie had fought side by side with white soldiers and only a year earlier he was working on plans for black and white veterans to work together, but he now found himself assigned by the Army to a segregated National Guard unit. He could not have thought of this as progress. Nevertheless, it was exciting to be training young black men (and other men of color) in an environment where the best that he had to offer would shine. Sergeant Carter was a challenging teacher, a true mentor, and an appealing older brother figure to dozens of young black men. He was an empowering model of dignified, competent, and self-confident manhood. He looked the part as well, with his immaculate, neatly pressed uniform, polished boots, chest emblazoned with medals. From a heroic warrior Eddie remade himself into an inspiring teacher. It gave him enormous satisfaction and pride.

In 1997, I met Neale Henderson when National Guard veterans invited me to speak about Eddie. Henderson was one of the young men Eddie had trained. "It was at Fort MacArthur, just outside of Los Angeles on the coast, that I first met Sergeant Carter when I went for my two weeks' training with the Guard. He gave us our basic training— marching, drilling, M1 rifle training, and so on. Later, at San Luis Obispo, he trained us in the use of heavy equipment. Then, at Camp Roberts, when we were called up for the regular Army, he trained us in how to put up steel

Eddie and Mildred at a club in Los Angeles after the war.

treadway bridges, how to build an abutment for the foundation and slope it properly. He taught us to operate bulldozers in road building, and put in gulleys and drainage. He trained us up in the mountains on thirty- and fifty- caliber machine guns, too. He was a hell of a guy. He could do it all. He was a soldier that I wanted to be like, and he taught me how to be a good soldier. With the training that he gave me, I soon made corporal and then sergeant in the Army.

"Another time at Camp Roberts," Henderson recalled, "we were laying a mine field, and he was showing us how to do the mapping of a mine field. Afterwards, he showed us how to breach a mine field with a special torpedo. Three of us were being trained. We put the torpedo in, we pulled the pin, and then we took off running. But this young recruit who was with us went down before we reached safety. When David McCoy and I saw that he was down, we turned and ran back to get him out of danger so he wouldn't get hurt. Sergeant Carter told us we did the right thing."

Eddie worked with the National Guard for a year and a half. During that time he and the other Army instructors succeeded in expanding the Guard from an under-manned, poorly prepared outfit into a full-fledged, well-trained military organization fully capable of being called up on a moment's notice for regular Army duty. This was a major accomplishment for which the Army instructors were largely responsible. Eddie knew that what they were doing was important and he took pride in their achievement. He had been determined to excel in this assignment, and he did. He was happy and so were his commanding officers. The black Army instructors had turned segregation in the National Guard to their advantage and proved that black officers and instructors could turn out top-notch soldiers and engineers.

Despite the appearance that all was going well, it was while he was serving as an instructor with the National Guard that Eddie discovered he was under surveillance. The men Eddie worked with also became aware of the surveillance. John Pulliams, an Army Air Force man who was assigned to work as an administrative assistant in the armory on Exposition Boulevard, recalled being questioned by a man from Army intelligence. "I remember *Ebony* magazine had published a big article that talked about Sergeant Carter," Pulliams said. "Carter was something of a celebrity. I got to know him when we worked at the National Guard Armory. He was a very quiet person, but he was a better soldier than me. One day in 1947 this man from Army intelligence came and asked me about Carter. Was he a communist? I said I never saw anything that indicated he was associated with any communist activity. So I knew they had him under surveillance, and sometimes I saw their cars parked outside."

Woodfred Jordan recounted an incident he witnessed. "Carter knew he was under some kind of surveillance. Sometimes when we were at [battalion instructor] Richardson's house, Carter would pull aside the curtains and look out the window. 'Come over here and look at this,' he'd say to us. 'See that car sitting there,' he'd say, pointing to a car parked on the street with men inside it wearing civilian clothes. 'They have me under surveillance.' He said they kept track of where he was. One time, he even walked outside and approached them, but they drove away."

The government's interest in black personnel in the California National Guard was not new. In 1944, according to an FBI report I found in the National Archives on alleged foreign-inspired agitation among blacks in Los Angeles, the FBI had at least one informant reporting on black California state Guard units. The informant, identified only as T-1, seemed especially interested in any weapons in possession of the all-black Seventh Battalion. "The officers of this [unit] wear side arms. The men carry rifles and machine guns," the report stated. "Informant T-1 advised that some of the officers take their side arms home; however, they are requested to unload them. They are required to turn in their machine guns and rifles at the armory before departing after drill."

The surveillance of Sergeant Carter continued. Eddie wrote later that he was constantly shadowed by two CIC (Army Counterintelligence Corps) agents wherever he went. At one point he was questioned by the agents. They asked about his attendance at the Welcome Home, Joe dinner. Eddie said he attended but he had no idea that the Communist Party was involved with the sponsoring organization.

Then, without warning, in July 1948, Eddie was abruptly removed from the National Guard and transferred to Fort Lewis in Washington state. Eddie said later that he was told by Colonel L. R. Boyd, the senior Army instructor and Eddie's immediate superior officer, that Boyd tried to keep him as an instructor with the Guard, but was rebuffed. General Mark Clark, commander of Sixth Army headquarters at San Francisco's Presidio and the top commander for the regular Army instructors, responded to Boyd's attempt at intervention by stating, "Whenever you are in doubt as to the loyalty of an individual, that individual must suffer."

CHAPTER SEVEN

STONEWALLED

From interviews with veterans I had learned much of the story of Eddie's experience in the National Guard, but my efforts to find documentation had been unsuccessful. The regular Army's records were in the National Archives, but not the records of the National Guard. Joe Wilson, a military historian whom I had met, referred me to a citizen-soldiers museum in Sacramento. In the museum's library I found a copy of the biennial report of the adjutant general of the state of California for the period from July 1, 1946, to June 30, 1948, the time frame during which Eddie was an instructor. Browsing through the report I grew excited when I came across a section dealing with the history of the 1401st and 1402d Engineers, battalions in the Sixth Engineer Combat Group with which Eddie had been an instructor.

At the end of the history of these units I found an appendix with lists of names. Jordan's name caught my eye first, then I saw Richardson and Pulliams. Eddie's name must be here somewhere, I thought, but I couldn't find it. I visited the California State Library and pored over more records, but still I found no mention of Sergeant Carter. It was as though Eddie had never been associated with the California National Guard. Had his name been deliberately purged?

My puzzlement led me to search for clues in Mildred's memorabilia. I had already sorted through everything in her trunk, but there were other boxes that had not been opened. In early March 1998, I once again found myself going through various boxes when I stumbled upon a letter from the American Civil Liberties Union addressed to a Dr. Nicholas Cunningham at an address in New York City. Dated December 9, 1958, the first sentence read: "I have given careful consideration to your letter addressed to Mr. Levy, who is now in private practice, and I have carefully reviewed our files on the Edward Allen Carter case." When I saw Eddie's name, I stopped cold. I didn't know anyone named Nicholas Cunningham or anything about an ACLU case.

The letter was from Rowland Watts, staff counsel of the ACLU. It read in part:

> As you know we were very interested in the matter when it first came to our attention at the end of 1949. We carried on extensive negotiations with the War Department over several years, both directly and through several Congressmen. We also took the matter up with the White House. We were completely

unsuccessful then and I am very much afraid that we would be equally unsuccessful now.

My mind was spinning as I read this. The references to the War Department and the White House were especially intriguing, and there was also mention of whether Eddie might be permitted to reenlist in the Army. When Buddha came home from work I asked him if he knew anything about an ACLU case. He didn't, but he did remember a person named Cunningham, a young white doctor who was a friend of Mildred's. He said Cunningham and Mildred worked at the same hospital in Los Angeles in the 1950s, and he remembered Cunningham coming to the house to hang out with Mildred and her friends. Eddie knew Cunningham, Buddha said, but they didn't seem to be close.

My guess was that Cunningham had learned about the 1949 ACLU involvement from Mildred and had decided to write to the ACLU about it. He must have given Mildred this letter so she would know the response.

The next day I called the ACLU and arranged to have the seventy-one-page case file sent to me. After reading the file I felt certain that Eddie had not knowingly done anything that could be considered disloyal or subversive. I knew it because he was fighting the Army with everything he had. And they were not giving him any reason or explanation as to why he was denied reenlistment. They refused to give him a hearing and they refused to give him any explanation. They were stonewalling him. The ACLU, in the person of Herbert Levy, who was then the organization's staff counsel, tried for more than five years to get something out of the Army, but all they got was bureaucratic bluster. Reading that case made me angry, but it also gave me the confidence to press ahead. I was no longer afraid of what I might find.

After Eddie was abruptly removed from the instructor group of the National Guard, he was assigned to the Military Police, Provost Detachment in Fort Lewis, Washington. The Provost Detachment was composed of about one hundred men, black and white, a large percentage of whom were combat veterans. Ironically, Eddie soon found himself working on drug cases that involved coordinating with military intelligence, the FBI, and local police in Tacoma. Apparently, the top brass at Fort Lewis did not know he was under suspicion; in any event, they assigned him to tasks as they saw fit. As usual, Eddie went at it with gusto and total commitment. On July 19, 1948, after working on a dangerous drug bust, he wrote to Mildred: "We have been working night and day on a dope case (marijuana). We captured the ring leader and all the small fry. We have been working with the CID [Army criminal investigation division], FBI, and civilian police. Last night I captured four men by myself with no gun play, although for a minute I almost was about to gun them down. I was working by myself, and I guess they thought I must be crazy being on the lone. The people up here gave us a writeup in the paper. If I can get the paper, I will send it along."

He was already thinking about having Mildred and the children come join him. He said that he could find an apartment, drive down to Roscoe, a Los Angeles suburb where the family was now living, and bring them all to Washington. Once again strapped for money—he earned $100 a month, almost all of which went to pay family bills—he suggested Mildred ask her aunt for a loan to help them make the move.

Money worries were not all that troubled Eddie and Mildred. Military counterintelligence was still snooping around, to Mildred's dismay. At the end of July he wrote to soothe Mildred: "Please do not let the CIC worry your pretty head. After all, my record is clean and I or you have nothing to fear. To me they seem to be a bunch of crazy loons. It's impossible. As for myself, I don't even attempt to try and understand them. . . . Regardless of their under-handed methods I will always be loyal and faithful to the United States government and Army. I am first and last an American soldier. And a darn good soldier."

Although the Counterintelligence Corps was still wor-risome, Eddie was winning praise from the base com-mander. "General Colins, the post commander, told all of the soldiers, both white and colored, that I was the only damn man that dressed, marched, and looked like a sol-dier," Eddie boasted to Mildred in August.

Interestingly, in this letter Eddie also mentioned that

General Mark Clark, the Sixth Army commander, was coming to Fort Lewis. Remembering how Mildred loved parades, he wrote with boyish glee that he wished Mildred could be there to see the show they would be putting on for the occasion. He assured her she would get her fill of parades once she moved to Washington. Of course, General Clark was the man who had expressed doubts about Eddie's loyalty when Eddie's commander in the National Guard protested his removal.

Perhaps Eddie had decided to forget the general's remark. He may have thought that he could leave his troubles in California. Things were going well for him at Fort Lewis. After only one month his skills as an instructor were recognized. "As of tomorrow," he wrote Mildred on August 13, 1948, "I will start training military police recruits. That means I will not have to pull town patrol."

Eddie's feelings for Mildred remained as strong as ever. "Darling, I love you so darn much that it frightens the hell out of myself," he told her in the same letter. "We have been a long time together, Mil. Let's grow old together. Okay darling? Okay. You will always be my girl."

Mildred was not only Eddie's great love, she was also his teacher. She showed him that love could be constant, no matter how much physical separation there might be between them. In a letter dated September 7, he wrote: "Each time we are forced apart only verifies my great need and love for you. These few years that we have been together [have] gradually softened this flint heart of mine. I have always been so afraid of love. You have given me your love so unselfishly—your love is what I need forever. . . . Please love me always darling. I need the two of you. I need you and I need love. And I promise to love also, to be so very much more thoughtful than I have been. . . . Let us always stay man and wife. Let us always continue to be lovers."

A few days later, on September 10, Eddie signed a lease with the Housing Authority of Tacoma for a three-bedroom apartment on Portland Avenue. Later he arranged for thirty-four items of household furniture, including a refrigerator, washing machine, two beds, two bicycles, a violin case, and several trunks, footlockers, and cartons of goods to be shipped to him at the military police station at Fort Lewis.

Eddie was tremendously excited about having his family join him. He requested a furlough so that he could return to Los Angeles to help with the move. He had more good news to report. In a letter dated September 24, he wrote, "I was ordered off the field today and told that I was to be the commanding general's bodyguard for Sunday. I believe that I have written before telling you that twice the general has picked me out as a soldier's soldier. I am considered to be the best-dressed soldier in the Military Police and the Second Infantry Division. I am well respected here on the post. I really believe that I will win out in the end. After all, you believe in me. So I couldn't very well let my sweetheart down, could I?" Eddie enjoyed the attention he was getting, which he regarded as

Happy times for Eddie and Mildred Carter in Tacoma, Washington, 1949.

reflecting his dedication as a soldier. He also understood the value of making a positive impression. "I have loads of equipment to take care of. Plenty of leather and brass to keep polished. I spend about one and a half to two hours a day just on the care of equipment. . . . Now my dear, I must prepare for tomorrow morning's inspection. I couldn't let my unit down or my commander."

By the spring of 1949, Eddie had settled his family in Tacoma and he was engaged in training infantry soldiers much as he had done in the California National Guard. Now promoted to sergeant first class and assigned to L

Company, Ninth Infantry Regiment, he was a platoon sergeant. As part of their training, thousands of soldiers from Fort Lewis were sent to the Yakima Firing Center, located in a remote, dusty, mountainous area, for two weeks of training exercises. The hazards of training ranged from avoiding rattlesnakes to demolition of unexploded artillery shells.

As the base artillery division returned to Fort Lewis from Yakima maneuvers in early May 1949, some 3,200 men of the Ninth Infantry arrived at Yakima to start two weeks of intensive field training. Reporting on these events in its Friday, May 13, issue, the base newspaper *The Flame-Spearhead* noted that the Ninth Infantry was one of the oldest regiments in the Army, having fought in the wars against the Indians before the Civil War.

In the same issue of the newspaper was a laudatory story on Sergeant Carter. The headline on the article declared, "Soldiering Natural Thing to Sgt. Who Served with Three Armies," and below it was a photo of an unsmiling Sergeant Carter in dress uniform looking at a swastika-emblazoned Nazi German flag. "A veteran of three armies and winner of the Distinguished Service Cross," the piece began, "the Ninth Infantry hails Sergeant Edward A. Carter as its most decorated Negro soldier."

The article summarized Eddie's background and his combat experiences in Asia and Europe. "Carter's war wounds have all healed now," the article ended. "Strangely

Sergeant Carter posing with the Nazi flag for an article
in the post newspaper at Fort Lewis, Washington, 1949.

enough the DSC winner isn't ready to quit yet. After fighting Japs, Spaniards and Jerries, he still remains in the Army. He plans to retire in about eleven years." This was the first disclosure I had found that Eddie intended to reenlist and pursue a career in the Army.

Interestingly, in the very same issue of *The Flame-Spearhead*, there was also a brief article announcing that an inspection team from the Sixth Army had arrived at Fort Lewis on May 8. "The inspection, conducted semiannu-

Sergeant Carter at Fort Lewis, Washington,
shortly before being denied reenlistment.

ally, includes an inspection of the General Reserve Units at Fort Lewis, Yakima, and Fort Worden," the article said. "The team is composed of four inspection groups: training, intelligence, administrative and logistics."

Since the Sixth Army commander was General Mark Clark, who had questioned Eddie's loyalty, and given that Army counterintelligence was still actively interested in Eddie's doings, it's clear with hindsight that this wasn't an ideal time for Eddie to announce his intention of reenlisting. But Eddie thought things were looking up.

In the fall of 1949, when his second tour of duty ended, Eddie found that he was not going to be welcomed back with open arms. The story of his dismissal was revealed in a seven-page letter dated December 5, 1949, that Eddie wrote to Herbert Levy of the ACLU asking for help.

> Sir, two days prior to my discharge a letter arrived [at Fort Lewis headquarters] from the Department of the Army, with the signature of Edward F. Witsell, Major General, the Adjutant General. One of my very good friends, an officer, called me into his office and I was shown this directive. This directive stated, 'Upon discharge of Edward A. Carter, Jr. . . . of your organization [he] is not to be reenlisted. Notation to be included on discharge: 'Not eligible for reentry into the Army unless authorized by the Adjutant General.' 'No interrogation authorized.' Sir, this officer explained that this directive was classified as confidential and that I was not to know about the above orders until my discharge September 21, 1949, two days later. Also, that whatever questions that I asked were to go unanswered.

Eddie must have left this meeting feeling great anger and confusion. The Fort Lewis officers apparently wanted

Eddie to know that this was not their doing, but that fact provided little consolation.

I try to imagine a distraught Eddie coming home that day to Mildred. She would have tried to comfort him, but I'm sure that Eddie was inconsolable. They both knew that Eddie didn't deserve this unjust dismissal. On the contrary, Eddie was held in high regard by every officer who had ever had Eddie in his unit. Sitting at the kitchen table together, they would have resolved to fight this underhanded action by the Army's high command. Mildred, I'm sure, offered to do whatever she could to help Eddie get Witsell's directive reversed.

As befits a man of action, Eddie decided to go straight to the top, and to make his case in person. The day his discharge was formally issued Eddie purchased a round-trip ticket to Washington, D.C. He left the next day from Tacoma.

Eddie presented himself at the Pentagon and asked for the opportunity to defend himself. He asked the Inspector General for a hearing. This was refused. Adjutant General Witsell refused to see him, as did Army intelligence. As a last resort he went to Clarence Mitchell, labor secretary of the National Association for the Advancement of Colored People.

Mitchell was encouraging, saying that he would look into the matter. He also suggested that Eddie write to the NAACP Legal Defense Fund in New York. The LDF was experienced in handling cases of mistreatment of black soldiers in the military. Still, Eddie left Washington feeling that he had not accomplished his mission. He had filed a written complaint with the Inspector General's office stating his willingness to undergo any test and to submit sworn statements to clear up any suspicion of alleged disloyalty, but in the end he felt that his trip to the Pentagon had been in vain. Eddie's son Redd remembered his father's return from Washington. "He had gone there to talk to the generals," Redd recalled, "but they wouldn't see him. That broke my father's heart. They were killing him slowly."

For his part Mitchell, immediately fired off a telegram to Secretary of Defense Louis Johnson inquiring about Sergeant Carter's case. Mitchell's telegram was passed through channels, eventually arriving on the desk of Adjutant General Witsell, whom Sergeant Carter had been unsuccessful in seeing during his visit. Witsell replied to Mitchell on November 4, stating his position that Carter's records had been carefully reviewed by competent Department of the Army agencies, and it was determined that his reenlistment could not be authorized.

The same nonexplanation was made in a separate letter from Witsell to Eddie. In October, Eddie had written to President Harry Truman about his plight, affirming his loyalty and willingness to defend the United States. He wrote that the Army had left him and his family stranded in Tacoma, and he asked for prompt action, as the family's small funds were growing smaller. The White House passed the letter to the Army, where it came to Witsell's desk for acknowledgment. Witsell's reply might as well have been a form letter. Apparently, all inquiries about Eddie were being forwarded routinely to Witsell for reply.

Mitchell, meanwhile, employed his lobbying skills and made sure the Pentagon knew that others were interested in Sergeant Carter's plight. Among those who took an early interest in Eddie's situation was Helen Gahagan Douglas, a staunch liberal and member of Congress from California. Mrs. Douglas asked for a hearing for Sergeant Carter. She said that surely someone who had served his country so bravely deserved to know the basis of the decision against him and should have the right to be heard in his own behalf.

A barrage of letters, calls, and telegrams was orchestrated by Mitchell. Another letter from Mitchell himself to the secretary of defense drew a rambling reply from James Evans, assistant to the secretary. Sounding peeved, Evans twice alluded to the many communications and telephone calls he had received as a result of Mitchell's efforts. These included, Evans wrote, White House Committees, members of Congress, the Department of Defense, the Department of the Army, the Office of the Adjutant General, the Federal Security Agency, and various members of the press. Evans admonished Mitchell that, despite suggestions to the contrary, his office had yet to find a direct racial factor in the difficulties encountered by Sergeant Carter.

Evans said the Carter case first came to the attention

of the secretary of defense's office in August. "It was recited that former Sergeant Carter wished to reenlist in the Army," Evans wrote, "and wanted to make the Army a career." What is interesting here is that the plans of a first sergeant to reenlist should be brought to the attention of the secretary of defense's office the month before his present enlistment ended. It seems that a rather high level of consultation was invoked in the process of deciding to bar Eddie from reenlisting.

While this correspondence was going on, Eddie and his family moved to an apartment on Vancouver Avenue in Tacoma. The family had to scramble to keep afloat. As soon as he returned from Washington, Eddie began looking for work. Here his old problem—lack of civilian job skills—confronted him again. Eddie tried his hand at various odd jobs to make ends meet. Mildred got work as a cleaner in a restaurant. Soon the family moved out of Tacoma to a small farm they rented in nearby Orting.

Although it was a difficult time for the family, the boys found life on a farm exciting. Redd remembers Eddie teaching them about farm life, while raising pigs, rabbits, and turkeys to supplement the family's income. "He also brewed a little beer on the side," Redd recalled. For Buddha, a high point was when his father, an expert marksman, taught the boys to shoot. While their parents worked, the boys attended the local elementary school. "My father wasn't a very affectionate person," Buddha

Edward "Buddha" Carter III and William Carter
with their pets on the farm in Orting, Washington, 1950.

recalled, "at least not toward us. But we knew he loved us. We knew it from the way he would talk with us and the things he taught us. He spent a lot of time with us. Ours was not a family with a lot of hugging and kissing, but everybody was comfortable, and we knew he really cared for us."

★   ★   ★

Although initially disheartened, Eddie grew more determined to fight the Army's refusal to let him reenlist or grant him a hearing. In November, two months after his denial, Eddie wrote to the NAACP Legal Defense Fund in New York for help. Jack Greenberg, then assistant to special counsel Thurgood Marshall, passed Sergeant Carter's request and materials on to the ACLU, saying "as far as we can determine there is no factor of racial discrimination present in this case. Carter's predicament seems to be of the customary loyalty species."

It fell to Herbert Levy to reply. Levy, a young graduate of Columbia University's law school and former ACLU legal volunteer newly appointed as staff counsel, asked what information Sergeant Carter had from the Army regarding the basis of their action. He said he would let Eddie know what the ACLU could do to help.

In reply to Levy's request, Eddie and Mildred sent the letter of December 5 giving details of his situation with the Army. The letter recounted Eddie's background, his service in three wars, his medals, his honorable discharge and reenlistment, and his service in the California National Guard. The seven-page letter, apparently dictated by Eddie but written in Mildred's flowing penmanship, continued: "Sir, from my second enlistment until my recent discharge I was constantly hounded by our 'Secret Police.' I was questioned about attending a 'Welcome

Home, Joe' dinner given under the auspices of the 'American Youth for Democracy.' At the time I was definitely ignorant that the above organization was a 'Red Front.' I was constantly shadowed by two C.I.C. agents wherever I went." Eddie told Levy of his sudden severance from the Guard, the comment by General Clark, and his transfer to Fort Lewis. Eddie added, "Sir, I have never belonged [to] or been a member of any organization that advocates the overthrow of our government through force or violence."

Summing up his military career to that point, Eddie wrote that he was an excellent soldier who was consistently selected to instruct other soldiers. "Soldiering is my profession," he said.

In the last two pages of that letter Eddie could not contain his anger. "During World War II, I believed that I was fighting a 'Holy War.' I believed and fought in defense of the democracy I now find myself denied. According to the laws of our democracy, an individual is innocent until proven guilty. According to the powers that be, that law has been interpreted in the opposite [way]. Should that be the case, I ask for the right in the name of democracy, that so many profess, to prove my loyalty and establish my innocence. I am not afraid to face any board of inquiry, in fact, I invite a hearing or trial."

The many decorations he had received were meaningless, an insult to one's intelligence, he wrote. More meaningful were the scars of battle that he would carry to his grave, scars received in defense of the democracy he was now denied. Instead of attempting to export democracy, Eddie wrote bitterly, the United States should try importing it.

Eddie ended his letter with a scathing denunciation of the police state he saw rising in the United States. Coming as it did on the eve of McCarthyism's cancerous flourishing, Eddie's letter was prophetic. "Sir, I believe that the people of our country do not realize how much the United States has become a 'Police State.' The very evils that we fought against in World War II were not destroyed. We have captured and adopted many of these evils. Sir, I shall continually fight for redress. I wish to be charged with whatever charges the Department of the Army has. Once again, I repeat, I invite any hearing or trial."

Eddie and Mildred were grasping for some way to confront an opponent who would not show his face or present any evidence of Eddie's wrongdoing. Instead, the Army preferred to use innuendo to smear Eddie's reputation and destroy the career of a person whose only crime was that he was a proud black man and a superb soldier. By the time I finished reading Eddie's letter I was angry myself.

Arthur Garfield Hays, Levy's boss at the ACLU, wrote to Army Adjutant General Edward Witsell on February 15, 1950, asking why Sergeant Carter was denied permission to reenlist despite his distinguished service record.

Hays said Carter thought it was because he attended a meeting of an alleged subversive nature. "Mr. Carter advised me that he had no information at the time that the meeting was of such a nature, and he further advises me that he never has had and does not now have any connection whatsoever with any organization on the subversive list." Hays ended his letter with a request for a hearing for Sergeant Carter.

Witsell's reply to Hays, if any, was not in the file. However, in a collection of materials I obtained later through the assistance of Kenneth Schlessinger at the National Archives, I found a draft of a letter from Witsell written in response to a November 15, 1950, follow-up query from Herbert Levy. Witsell acknowledged that the Army had received many requests from individuals and agencies asking that Sergeant Carter be allowed to reenlist. Witsell again repeated his assertion that a careful review of the case led to the determination that reenlistment could not be authorized. His letter ended: "I am obliged to advise you that the information in this case is classified investigative material, and that for this reason your request must be respectfully denied."

There would be no reenlistment, no further explanation or information, no hearing. Witsell's draft letter was passed on to the secretary of the army and the White House as the suggested reply to any future inquiries about Sergeant Carter. No inquiry would be allowed to get beyond this stonewalling form-letter response.

For Eddie and his family, conditions had worsened. On May 2, he wrote to Levy that after word got around that he had been kicked out of the Army as an alleged communist he had lost two jobs. Eddie was angry. "I find it hard to make a living for my wife and four children. The only profession that I am familiar with is that of a soldier. How to kill and not be killed. Perhaps military tactics will prove successful against a bank or two."

Instead of robbing a bank Eddie took a more heartbreaking step. After seven months of waiting, he was losing hope of gaining redress, he wrote. He had lost faith and was disappointed in American democracy. Politicians could get hearings, he said, but he, an ordinary citizen, could not. Enclosed with the letter was Eddie's Distinguished Service Cross. He asked Levy to return the medal to President Harry S. Truman. In his country's hour of need, Eddie ended, he was in the front lines with a submachine gun in his hand. "My reward? A stab in the back."

Levy was deeply disturbed by Eddie's letter, with the enclosed medal. "I was stunned," he later recalled. "This man had more than earned this medal, I thought. He should keep it, not give it back." In his reply to Eddie, Levy sought to give the matter a positive spin. He said he would keep the medal in case a direct appeal to the President and a full-scale publicity campaign became necessary. For Levy, Sergeant Carter's case was a matter of common decency and justice.

After more unsuccessful appeals for help to Secretary of Defense Louis Johnson, politicians, and the press, Levy sensed that that his efforts were not going to succeed. Eddie, too, was feeling despondent.

Levy appealed for help to David Niles, administrative assistant to President Truman. Niles replied on February 26, 1951, that he had been familiar with the case "for some time," having queried James Evans in the secretary of defense's office in response to a call on Eddie's behalf from Congresswoman Helen Gahagan Douglas. "I received the answer," Niles wrote, "that Carter had been denied the right of reenlistment on security reasons, which were based on confidential information that could not be disclosed. The Army is, of course, entirely within its rights in setting conditions for reenlistment—in this case, for security reasons."

Two years later, in March 1953, Eddie wrote to ask if Levy thought there might be a better chance under the new administration of Dwight Eisenhower. With McCarthyism in full swing, Levy was not optimistic. Nevertheless, he said he would take the issue up with the new administration.

Again there was to be no success. Over the next two years there were occasional letters between Eddie and Levy. In May 1954, Eddie wrote that he was forced to concede defeat. He asked Levy to return all papers and his Distinguished Service Cross. Levy responded that although he was pessimistic, he would not admit defeat.

But in the end Levy did return all of Eddie's papers and his Distinguished Service Cross. The return of these materials meant the end of any hope of redress. "After looking at the Cross," Eddie told Mildred, "I almost broke down and cried. That Army deal I took harder than anything I ever had to. You'll never realize just how tough it was on me."

As it became apparent that the ACLU case had gotten nowhere, the family decided to return to Los Angeles with the hope of making a new start. The farm in Orting, while a pleasant interlude for the boys, was not economically viable. Both Eddie and Mildred held down jobs in Tacoma to make ends meet. In June 1954, they decided that Mildred and the boys would return to Los Angles to live with Mildred's parents. Eddie was doubtful that he could find work in Los Angeles, so he decided to stay in Washington working to pay off the family's accumulated debts. He rented a room in the home of friends. To Eddie, this separation must have seemed liked another defeat. It was a separation that would last for a year and a half.

During this long separation Eddie and Mildred wrote to each other faithfully, as they had during the war years. Mildred, as she had done before, saved all of Eddie's letters. Their main concern was to reduce their debt and reunite the family. In almost every letter Eddie reported that he was paying off the bills as they planned. He often sent money to Mildred as well. He reported on his work

Eddie (second from right) at work as a tire vulcanizer in 1950 in Tacoma, Washington, after being banned from the Army.

situation and his hopes of getting to Los Angeles soon. "All I am doing is working like the devil and coming back to my room," he wrote. "I do not go anywhere at all." Eddie found work with an automotive supply and service company in Tacoma. It was a union job—he was a member of the Teamsters Union—but the work was not always certain. Still, he managed to keep bill payments current. From time to time, he asked Mildred to watch for work in Los Angeles, but he was not optimistic.

Eddie was determined to pay off the debts before

164 ★ HONORING SERGEANT CARTER

coming to Los Angeles. But Mildred was pressing him to set a date for rejoining the family. "I shall be home just as soon as possible," he told her sharply in one letter. "So please don't make it any harder for me. Dammit! There are bills to pay. Do you have a job for me? Shinning shoes? Washing dishes? Cooking in someone's kitchen? No? Then you'll just have to wait."

When Mildred protested the tone of his letter, Eddie tried to smooth things over: "Darned if you didn't detect the ice in my letter. Oh, how I love you for you." But the longer the separation lasted, the more the tension built between them. By May 1955, they had been apart for nearly a year. Eddie sensed that Mildred was making a life for herself in Los Angeles, and he felt a need to reassert his control. "In your letters you write that you never have any time. And that you are always on the run. Do you think that you need a husband? Do you think that you will ever have any time to be a wife? You seem to be loving and living the life and the pace that you have set. When I return I intend stepping in on some of these people. In other words I intend telling them that you are my wife and not a social butterfly. Make up your mind now because I do not intend running around all over town. Now and then okay."

Eddie's growing edginess toward Mildred was compounded by health problems. On May 25, he complained of having bad headaches. "I just about go blind," he wrote. His war wounds also started acting up. He wrote

Mildred in July that his left arm, which had been wounded in the war, was giving him such pain that it kept him awake at night.

In September, Eddie was counting the days until he would be with his family. By then Mildred was working at the Los Angeles County Hospital as an aide and their financial situation was looking better. "Fifty-one more days until my last day of work up here," Eddie wrote on October 26. Then on December 2 he happily proclaimed: *"All bills are paid off."* He would work for two more weeks, he said, to pay for a plane ticket to Los Angeles. He didn't want a big group to meet him at the airport—only Mildred, her daughter Iris, and Iris's boyfriend Fred Scott would be there. In the final days before his departure Eddie told Mildred, "I still love you very much. It seems as though we are staring all over again. But we will and must make it."

Eddie finally rejoined his family at Mildred's parents' home in Los Angeles in December 1955. Her parents now lived in a big, rambling, two-story house on South Bonnie Brae that had five bedrooms, a full dining room, and a music room with a piano. The peaceful household of Mildred's parents now became home to Mildred and Eddie, four children, two Great Danes, a miniature Doberman pinscher, two adult Siamese cats, and several kittens. In a sense, for Eddie and Mildred, moving back into her parents home was a return to their beginnings, but not an altogether happy project.

Mildred's job at the county hospital gave the family an economic foothold. Eddie, with the help of a letter of recommendation from his former employer in Tacoma, found work as a tire vulcanizer. "He worked at a tire recapping plant on Jefferson Boulevard," Fred Scott recalled. "I remember seeing him come home in white coveralls that were soiled by the dirty work he had to do at that plant." To Eddie, whose pride had been manifested in an immaculate military uniform with sergeant's stripes and medals for bravery, ending each day in dirty coveralls would have represented another blow to his dignity. For Mildred, the return to Los Angeles had allowed her to resume the kind of social life she had always enjoyed. Old and new friends were frequent visitors at the house. Eddie, on the other hand, seemed more distant, and he made few friends.

Among Mildred's new friends was Nicholas Cunningham, the young doctor who later wrote to the ACLU on Eddie's behalf. He and Mildred shared an interest in music, and Cunningham often came to the house to visit with Mildred's family and friends.

Cunningham remembered Mildred as a charming, attractive, bubbly person. "I really liked her family," he recalled, "and for me it was like a home away from home. It was a very attractive, friendly environment. Sometimes we would play music together. She played violin and I played cello. Her youngest son, Redd, was really terrific—ebullient, talented, and very interested in sax and jazz.

Buddha, the oldest son, played alto sax, but he seemed a bit preoccupied, as if he was worried." Cunningham recalled Eddie as "a quietly intense person who was completely his own man. He didn't feel a need to prove anything to anybody."

If Buddha seemed worried to Cunningham, it was not without reason. When Eddie joined the family in Los Angeles, Buddha recalled, he "seemed more quiet and withdrawn. His spirit was different. It was like something had been taken away from him, but I didn't know what."

Redd also noticed the change. "Eddie was pulling away from us. Maybe he figured we were old enough and could handle ourselves. He spent a lot of time in his room reading. He loved to read magazines like *Popular Mechanics*. He didn't like a lot of noise, and we knew not to bother him."

Mildred also sensed a shift in Eddie's spirit, but she didn't talk about it. Still, the boys were aware of a difference in their parents' relationship. "My father and mother never had a fight in front of us," Redd said, "but things changed between them. I noticed that sometimes when they talked, it seemed like something didn't go right. I can't really pinpoint what it was. But my father would go upstairs and my mother stayed downstairs. She seemed to be hurt."

Over the following years Eddie developed noticeable health problems. A heavy smoker, he was often photographed with a cigarette perched on his lips. He was particularly fond of miniature Italian cigars.

Eddie also sometimes exhibited strange behavior. "I remember one night he called me into his room," Redd recalled. "I saw that he had two guns on the bed, a .357 magnum pistol and a big rifle that looked something like an M1 rifle only it wasn't. 'What's all this,' I said. 'I'm working as a security guard,' he said. 'Well, I'd be worried about any guys breaking in . . . ,' I started to say because I knew he could shoot. I once saw him shoot a crow out of a tree a long way off, and he told us exactly where the bullet had entered and exited before we retrieved the crow's body—and he was right. He picked up the .357 magnum and gave it to me. 'Pull the trigger,' he said. 'Eddie, you trained me never to pick up a gun unless I intend to use it,' I said. 'So I'll put this back on the bed because I don't intend to use it.' He put the guns away. He seemed so different. I didn't know what to make of this, but I believe he was thinking about dying. Maybe he even wanted to die. I didn't know it then, but in fact he was already dying."

Eddie was diagnosed with lung cancer. He was taken to the hospital for cobalt treatments, but his condition worsened rapidly. Within a matter of weeks, on January 30, 1963, Sergeant Edward A. Carter Jr. died at age forty-six.

On learning of Eddie's death, Fred Scott recalled thinking of the spirit who had told Eddie he would be a great warrior and survive many wounds so long as he protected his chest. "I wondered if the spirit whispered in his ear, 'I didn't say to protect yourself just on the battlefield.'"

★   ★   ★

On a rainy day, appropriately, he was buried at the Veterans Cemetery near UCLA. Mildred, the boys, and a small group of family and friends attended the ceremony. His brother William was there, but Miriam, his sister, had died three years earlier. His father, the evangelist, eighty-six years old and by then blind, did not attend because of his failing health. Eddie was buried in his old Army uniform, with his medals on his chest and, in a sense, the memory of who he had been.

CHAPTER EIGHT

A HERO VINDICATED

Eddie Carter was a fading memory by the time I married his son in 1973. By then his presence had been replaced by a deep silence that would not be disturbed until Gloria Long's telephone call more than thirty-three years after his death. My long and sometimes puzzling quest to discover what had happened to Eddie was often exasperating, producing more questions than answers. Finally, in April 1999, a critical piece of the puzzle finally fell into place—Eddie's almost forgotten Freedom of Information Act file arrived in the mail.

The packet, in response to my request in January 1997, contained more than sixty pages of documents. As I began looking through the files I was worried that, despite my confidence that Eddie hid nothing and had done nothing wrong, there might be some shock awaiting me in this material. I had already experienced many surprises, sometimes upsetting, in my research. So I braced myself as I began going through the files.

In the files were memos and correspondence, most pertaining to an investigation of Eddie by Army intelligence in 1942 and 1943, when Eddie was assigned to an all-black service battalion at Fort Benning in Georgia. The investigation was opened on October 1, 1942, according to a local military intelligence officer, "when it was learned that the Subject [Carter] had served in" the Abraham Lincoln Brigade. Investigators subsequently reviewed personnel files Eddie had filled out when he enlisted in 1941—which were destroyed in a fire in 1973— and they found detailed information about his childhood in India and China and his combat experience in Spain.

The Army investigators interviewed officers and enlisted men who worked with Eddie, and found nothing questionable in his behavior or words. Military agents checked police, court, and credit records. They interviewed his father in Los Angeles as well as former landlords, employers, and acquaintances. They examined the records of the House Un-American Activities Committee and found nothing on Eddie there. Everyone they interviewed spoke favorably of Eddie. No one had ever heard him express disloyal views or, for that matter, political opinions of any sort. Nevertheless, reports had to be written and passed to higher-ups. A report to the Military Intelligence Division in the War Department summarized what it referred to as "adverse information" on Eddie:

ADVERSE INFORMATION:

1. Subject reportedly was a member of Abraham Lincoln Brigade, having served for two and a half years with said Brigade in Spain.

A HERO VINDICATED ★ 173

2. Potentially adverse—Subject is seemingly potentially capable of having connections with subversive activities due to the fact that he spent his early years in the Orient and has a speaking knowledge of Hindustani and Mandarin Chinese.

3. Potentially adverse—Subject's father resides at 115 Shanse Road, Shanghai, China and Subject's mother (name not available) was born in Calcutta, India; but no data is available as to whether she is living or deceased.

It was notable that Eddie's service with the Abraham Lincoln Brigade was "adverse information" even though an earlier report had stated that members of the brigade were "not necessarily Communists." And I can almost see the intelligence agent puzzling over the unusual circumstances of this "colored" soldier's upbringing and deciding that Eddie could somehow be connected with subversive activities. This unfounded speculation, a totally improper exercise of the agent's imagination, was based on nothing more than the agent's preconceptions and biases. But the agent's speculation was now part of the rationale for investigating Eddie. The memo concluded: "Subject's loyalty to the United States seemingly is unquestioned except as regards his background, but due to his former connections with above mentioned organization, it is thought that a more thorough investigation into Subject's loyalty should be made."

I was not altogether surprised to see that this information was forwarded directly to J. Edgar Hoover, director of the Federal Bureau of Investigation. I knew from my earlier research that Hoover's FBI had a great interest in suspected subversives in the black population and employed spies to track the activities of African Americans, most of which appeared to me, from their own reports, to be simply civil rights activism. Nevertheless, this memo to Hoover suggested that the FBI and Army intelligence were collaborating in this investigation of Eddie from the very beginning.

Five times in the reports it was recommended that the case be closed and that Eddie's records be marked "considered loyal." Finally, on June 24, 1943, a report to the War Department declared, "Recommend no further action be taken. Case CLOSED."

But the case was not closed, or perhaps it was periodically reopened. Eddie was under surveillance when he served as a trainer in the California National Guard. This was even indirectly admitted by General Mark Clark when he made his ominous when-loyalty-is-doubted-the-individual-must-suffer remark. Eddie also fell under suspicion at Fort Lewis in Washington. All of this culminated in him being denied reenlistment.

Then I saw the pattern. In each instance when there was a flurry of suspicion, investigation, and trouble for Eddie, it followed in the wake of publication of a news article about him in an Army newspaper. The first instance occurred a year after Eddie first enlisted. The Fort Benning post newspaper, *The Pine-Bur,* profiled Eddie. The article mentioned his life in China and fighting on the Loyalist side in Spain. The day the article was published, October 1, 1942, a surveillance file on Eddie was opened by the local intelligence officer. The second instance happened after the October 20, 1946, publication of a front-page article with photograph of Eddie in the *Lee Traveller* at Fort Lee, Virginia. The laudatory article focused on Eddie's heroism in the war, but it, too, mentioned China and Spain. At the beginning of 1947, when Eddie got back to California and joined the Army instructor group of the National Guard, he and others discovered that he was under surveillance, and he was later removed from the instructor group. This was also after the *Ebony* magazine article appeared. Finally, after being transferred to Fort Lewis in Washington, Eddie ran into trouble again. This time the trouble—denial of reenlistment—followed the appearance of another laudatory article with photograph in the May 13, 1949, issue of *The Flame-Spearhead,* the post newspaper.

In all of the Army newspaper articles, Eddie mentioned his early life in India and China, and his service with the Loyalists in the Spanish Civil War. Apparently this was enough to provoke a knee-jerk reaction from military intelligence and perhaps higher-ups, as though they

had just discovered a spy in their midst. If the conse-
quences hadn't been so hurtful to Eddie, this all could
have made an amusing episode of the Keystone Kops.
But it did harm him, and there was a mean-spirited intent
behind his persecution.

It became perfectly clear that the whole case against
Sergeant Carter was a fabrication when I read the last
document in the Freedom of Information Act file. It was
a memo from the G-2 intelligence service of the Army to
the director of the FBI, dated December 4, 1950, apparently in response to a query from the FBI about evidence
supporting the allegation that Sergeant Carter was a
Communist Party member. The memo said they had
nothing: "Information on the allegation is not reflected in
the files" of G-2.

I knew the 1942–1943 investigation of Eddie was
closed due to lack of evidence, but here was a document
suggesting that a new investigation had been initiated
after the war when Eddie reenlisted in the Army. Significantly, the source of the allegation was given as the Sixth
Army, which was General Mark Clark's command.
Knowing his attitude, I had suspected Clark might be one
of those behind the persecution of Eddie. This memo
added to my suspicion. But what was most infuriating was
the realization that this memo was sent in December
1950, a year after Eddie had sought help from the ACLU.
Herbert Levy had been told that on the basis of so-called
confidential information, Eddie could not be permitted to

reenlist for security reasons. Yet here was proof that Hoover, the FBI, Army intelligence, and probably the secretary of defense all knew that no such confidential information existed! And even after this memo was sent, David Niles, on advice of the Army, repeated Witsell's "security reasons . . . confidential information" smoke screen in a letter to the ACLU's Herbert Levy.

I now knew that there had been a concerted and continuing cover-up to hide the fact that there was no evidence against Eddie. A hearing might have brought this out—so no hearing could be allowed. This was cruel. Not only was Eddie prevented from reenlisting, but insinuations of disloyalty were continually leveled at him throughout his efforts to learn the truth. The institution that he so faithfully and heroically served, the U.S. Army, had betrayed him cruelly. In the end, it destroyed him and wounded his family. Sergeant Edward A. Carter Jr. was a casualty of the U.S. Army, and specifically of General Mark Clark.

Who was Mark Clark, and why would he have gone after Eddie? Clark wrote two memoirs: *Calculated Risk*, about his World War II experiences, and *From the Danube to the Yalu*, about his "running battle with the Communists from 1945 on," according to the jacket copy. Two other books, *Mark Clark: The Last of the Great World War II Commanders*, a biography by Martin Blumenson, and *Army Surveillance in America, 1775–1980*, by Joan M. Jensen, were also eye-openers that gave me insight into Clark and the strange history of the Army's Military Intelligence Division.

Military intelligence has a convoluted history going back to the American Revolution. The Russian Revolution of 1917 heightened the Army's interest in potential domestic enemies—radicals of various kinds, including Bolsheviks, communists, socialists, anarchists, labor leaders, and others. The Army pushed hard to persuade Congress to fund peacetime spying on civilians. In the summer of 1919, race riots occurred in Washington and Chicago. The riots left dozens dead and hundreds injured, mostly black people. The Military Intelligence Division (MID), seeking to bolster its case in Congress, seized on the riots as evidence that foreign-influenced radicals were inflaming black communities and inciting insurrections. Black undercover agents hired by the Justice Department said the riots were caused by homegrown injustice, not radical agitators, but the media played up white fears of black rebellion and the die was cast. Military surveillance of civilians was accepted as necessary, despite the objections of dissenters, to protect the nation's security and tranquillity.

On the civilian side, a young assistant in the Justice Department, J. Edgar Hoover, was put in charge of the new Radical Division. Hoover, who later became head of the new Federal Bureau of Investigation, launched a series of raids against suspected communists and worked closely with military intelligence to cultivate a climate of national hysteria and racism. A pattern of sharing information between military intelligence and the FBI developed, as I was to see when I obtained Eddie's Freedom of Information files. Occasional efforts by Congress to halt or limit civilian surveillance were effectively subverted by MID and the FBI, as they continued their unholy crusade against "radicals."

In 1921, in a period of criticism and reform, the name of MID was changed to G-2. But G-2 continued the practice of civilian surveillance, sometimes in direct violation of orders from Washington. G-2 would later spawn the Counterintelligence Corps, the agency responsible for much of the surveillance of Sergeant Carter.

Mark Clark, the son of a career Army officer, was an ambitious officer who swiftly rose into the ranks of the generals. With the help of his aunt Zettie, the mother of General George C. Marshall, he secured an appointment to the U.S. Military Academy at West Point, where he had a rather undistinguished record. Nevertheless, his connection with powerful men (Marshall, Eisenhower, and later Truman) would assure his rise to the highest levels of the Army.

Clark's career was marked by controversy and criticism. As Blumenson, his biographer, wrote:

> Some of his critics were jealous of his rapid rise in
> rank. As a lieutenant colonel in 1940, he passed over
> thousands of officers who were senior to him in age
> and length of service. By V-E Day he had moved up

five grades and wore the four stars of a general. Too quick a climb, they said, to learn thoroughly the profession of arms.

General Patton, Blumenson wrote, had grave reservations about Clark.

In private, Patton referred scathingly to Clark. In numerous diary entries and letters to his wife, Patton castigated Clark as "very clever and indirect," "too damned slick," and simply "an s.o.b." So far as Patton could tell, Clark had neither interest in nor understanding of soldiers and warfare. To Patton, what concerned Clark above all was Clark.

Problems in Clark's commands were not unknown. For example, serious charges were made that Clark's failure of leadership was responsible for the nearly 1,700 casualties suffered by the Thirty-sixth Division in an ill-considered and disastrous attempt to cross the Rapido River in Italy. Other troops under Clark's Fifth Army command included the all-black Ninety-second Division. According to Daniel Gibran and his colleagues, writing in *The Exclusion of Black Soldiers from the Medal of Honor,* the Ninety-sixth was accused by white officers of poor performance due to alleged racial characteristics of black soldiers, with the result that few awards for heroism were recommended for division members. Professor Gibran and his colleagues instead suggested that racial discrimination was a factor in fewer awards being recommended.

In *Calculated Risk,* published in 1950, Clark sought to distance himself from overt racists. "The 92nd Division performed a useful role," Clark wrote, "and its presence on Italy's west coast assisted us materially in our final drive into the Po Valley." But Clark argued that black soldiers were beset by serious handicaps of leadership and training, and he opposed the "indiscriminate mixing of Negro and white soldiers in our Army." Instead, he found acceptable the idea of including smaller all-black units within larger white combat units. This was the sort of modified segregation experienced by Eddie and the black combat volunteers in World War II.

As for Clark's racial views, his biographer reported that "Quite a few Americans found [Clark's] postwar activities distasteful, and they termed his political views as 'just this side of Genghis Khan' and deplored his close association with conservative politicians who opposed the extension of civil rights and the integration of blacks into the military services." Blumenson felt that Clark was a target of "largely unfair" criticism, but his book makes clear that Clark was obsessed with the idea that the United States was the victim of a gigantic communist conspiracy that was responsible, among other things, for promoting "intermarriages of the races, all the things that are bad for our country."

It was this attitude—his obsession with a "communist conspiracy" and the belief that civil rights activism was part of a communist plot—that linked Mark Clark to the prevailing ideology of the Military Intelligence Division, G-2, and the Counterintelligence Corps. Indeed, in his career, Clark, on two occasions, worked directly with G-2. In the early 1930s, while posted to the Seventh Corps Area in Omaha, Nebraska, Clark served as G-2's assistant chief of staff for intelligence. Later, in 1937, when stationed at Fort Lewis, Clark again served as assistant chief of G-2 in charge of intelligence.

Clark's anticommunism rigidified during his conflicts with the Russians in Austria after World War II and became an obsession during the Korean War, as is evident in his book *From the Danube to the Yalu.* "I was to learn that no matter the color of the skin, the sound of the language or the place of the meeting, a Communist anywhere was just the same as every other Communist." Clark felt that the communists had successfully recruited many American soldiers—even outstanding combat soldiers—into their ranks.

> Our agents learned that some . . . of the soldiers received their Communist Party orders at the beginning of their service in the American Army. The orders were for these men to prepare themselves for postwar leadership among their buddies by striving to become outstanding combat soldiers. This would

be evidence of patriotism as well as win them the admiration of their fellow soldiers.

It was evident from this that not only was Eddie suspect because of his association with the Abraham Lincoln Brigade, but in Mark Clark's eyes virtually everything about Eddie's Army and civilian careers was cause for suspicion. I thought of Eddie's struggle to succeed in the Army, his rise to sergeant, his volunteering for combat duty, his heroism in Germany, his return to the United States and his expression of hopes for peace and an end to racial discrimination, his plan to work with veterans, his work in the National Guard, his hope to pursue an Army career—and I realized that all of this would have been seen as evidence of Eddie's involvement in a communist plot in Mark Clark's twisted perspective. All of this would have made Eddie guilty and deserving of banishment.

Clark returned from Europe in June 1947 to be posted as commander of the Sixth Army headquartered at the Presidio in San Francisco, where he remained through 1949. Clark's thinly disguised racism and his overt obsession with communist plots became focused on Eddie when they both arrived in California after the war. Among other things, the Sixth Army was responsible for assisting in the upgrading and training of the California National Guard. Eddie probably came to the attention of Army counterintelligence as a result of articles about him in the *Lee Traveller* and *Ebony* magazine, and was soon placed under surveillance. But any investigation would have come to the attention of the Sixth Army commander, General Clark. The surveillance turned up nothing derogatory, as I now knew from the Freedom of Information file, but Eddie was abruptly detached from the Army instructor group and transferred to Fort Lewis. Eddie's immediate superior, Colonel L. R. Boyd, the Army's senior instructor, had no reason to have him transferred, and opposed it. The transfer would have been authorized by Clark. He may have regarded this as punishment, given his suspected-disloyalty-must-be-punished remark—and it was. Eddie was removed from an elite group of instructors who were successfully transforming the California National Guard into an effective force. Their success was becoming recognized within the military and among the public, but Eddie's removal would deny him any glory, instead leaving a cloud of suspicion and confusion, and even his name would be stricken from the record of this historic reconstruction of the National Guard. Perhaps General Clark thought that by removing Eddie from a high-profile unit and banishing him to Fort Lewis, that would be the end of him.

But Eddie did his best in every assignment given to him. At Fort Lewis he performed well as a military police officer, was soon assigned to be an instructor, and was praised by the base commander as "a soldier's soldier." Eddie was also promoted to sergeant first class. He believed that things were back on track, and that important opportunities would open up for him. Instead, a few months after the laudatory *Flame-Spearhead* article, he was denied the right to reenlist. The letter banning him from the Army came from Edward Witsell, adjutant general of the Army, but the process had to begin with the Sixth Army. Eddie's immediate superiors at Fort Lewis were pleased with him and had no reason to oust him from the Army. By this time Clark must have known there was no evidence against Eddie, but he was determined that Sergeant Carter, this audacious, proud black soldier who shone wherever he was assigned, must be brought down. Clark had the motive, the opportunity, and the power to destroy Eddie.

Ironically, as the process of Eddie's banishment was unfolding, the Army was in the midst of a campaign to improve the treatment of black soldiers and increase reenlistment. In 1946, the Army adopted a policy that required greater utilization of Negro soldiers "on a broader professional scale." President Truman's historic 1948 executive order desegregating the military, and offering equal treatment and opportunity to blacks in the military, further extended the shift in policy. With the growing need for labor power following the postwar demobilization, the Army launched a campaign to increase reenlistment, including black soldiers. Yet internal Army memoranda revealed that, in 1949, the Sixth Army under General Clark's command was resisting Army policy and seeking to limit black reenlistment and give preferential treatment to white soldiers who wanted to reenlist. Clark's resistance negatively impacted overall reenlistment rates. At Fort Lewis in the months before Eddie was barred from reenlistment, one report tellingly noted that the rate had dropped to an unexpectedly low level for "unknown" reasons. Army Chief of Staff General Omar Bradley, citing the shortage of high-quality men, wrote to Clark urging him to "maintain interest in the reenlistment drive." But while Clark claimed that he was working to implement policy and improve reenlistment rates, his treatment of black soldiers in general, and Eddie in particular, revealed a pernicious racial tilt.

Reprehensible behavior on the part of General Clark and his subordinates did not, however, relieve the Army or the government from responsibility for the injustice that was done to Eddie and the cover-up that followed. The fact is that many highly placed individuals were in a position to know what was going on, including Adjutant General Edward Witsell, FBI director J. Edgar Hoover, Secretary of Defense Louis Johnson, and Johnson's assistant, James Evans. This raises the question of the role played by Truman's assistant, David Niles. Did the President know the truth or was he lied to?

I told Buddha about the Freedom of Information Act file. It showed that they never had evidence to support the allegations against Eddie, I said, and they knew it all along. What could we do now, we wondered. Then Buddha said something that revealed what had to be done. The Medal of Honor was important, he said, but unless Eddie's name was cleared the medal was an honor without honor. "If they destroyed him before the world," he said, "let them apologize before the world." My initial response was skepticism: "That's all very noble but how do we get them to do that?" I couldn't imagine getting the Army to apologize. I scoffed at the idea—but then I started to think about it.

I recalled all the press furor at the time of the Medal of Honor events, and the anxiety of the White House and the military brass about how the press would handle the story. That experience gave me an appreciation of the importance and power of the media.

I thought of Joe Galloway, the *U.S. News & World Report* reporter who had written about the Medal of Honor awards. He impressed me as a fair and astute journalist and a sympathetic person. Was it possible that he would help us? I called him at his office in Washington and told him that there was a new development in the story of Sergeant Carter. He asked if I could fax the material to him. I wanted to whet his appetite. "Oh, I can't send this," I said. "It might be too hot to handle." That got his attention.

"Okay, what do you want to do?" he responded.

"Let's meet," I said. "I will come to Washington."

I put together a thick binder of the materials from the

188 ★ HONORING SERGEANT CARTER

files I had collected and an album of photographs. A few days later I flew to Washington. We met in a big conference room. Joe was there with his editor and a photographer and some other people. I was impressed; I had expected only to meet briefly with him. I laid out the material I had brought on the big conference table, and then I made my pitch about the mistreatment of Sergeant Edward Carter. I gave them a full summary of all that I had discovered.

By the time I finished, they were stunned. Joe suggested that I go to lunch while they decided what to do. Then he added that he would have a car pick me up at my hotel later because he wanted to do a photo shoot with me at Arlington National Cemetery, where Eddie now was buried. Now I was the one left waiting in suspense.

The photo shoot took place at Arlington at dusk. Joe Galloway was already working on the story. Before I left the magazine's office he was thinking of people to interview. Every name he mentioned—Herbert Levy, Russell Blair, and so on—I had included in a list of contacts with phone numbers and addresses in the binder I left with him. When I returned to the office Joe told me they had decided to revamp their planned Memorial Day issue and to instead use Eddie's story as the lead. It meant writing a ten-page feature story on short notice. It meant Eddie's picture would appear on the cover of the magazine. I couldn't have asked for anything more. "And we'll pay your expenses," Joe added, to my thankful relief.

Joe Galloway worked hard and fast on that story. I somewhat reluctantly left him my files, which I felt rather protective about, but they enabled him to write the story in the office with only a few phone calls. The whole staff, from top management on down, got on board for this story.

The timing was critical. It was published in the May 31, 1999, issue of *U.S. News & World Report*. I was thrilled to see the full-page photo of Eddie on the cover and the long, detailed article, with many more pictures inside the magazine. Because it was appearing in a national magazine on Memorial Day, the story came to the attention of hundreds of thousands of people, from ordinary citizens to high government officials. This was a story, the article began, "about how a battlefield hero could be broken by the country he served, then banished from his beloved military career like a bum." After recounting Eddie's heroism and posthumous Medal of Honor, it told of the covert suspicions and investigation and his long and unsuccessful effort to confront his accusers and clear his name. My efforts to find answers about what happened to Sergeant Carter were summarized. The article ended:

> Most of the answers are spread on the record, thanks to Allene Carter's bulldog tenacity. . . . What happened to Eddie Carter Jr. should never have happened in a democratic nation. . . . If the U.S. Army and the United States government would like to say

"We're sorry; we apologize for what happened to Eddie Carter," the Carter family says it is ready to listen and ready to forgive. And maybe a long-dead hero who now sleeps in Arlington National Cemetery will rest a bit easier.

This story got national attention, and other media—radio, television, other newspapers—started picking it up. Our phones were ringing off the hook.

The first public consequence of this flurry of activity was dramatic: a letter of apology from President Clinton.

This was a huge victory in our drive to clear Eddie's name. I was deeply grateful for the President's swift action. His letter lifted the spirits of our family and everyone else who wished to see justice done. His letter also gave a strong impetus to others, such as the Board for Correction of Military Records, to review the case.

I had never approached the Board for Correction of Military Records because I didn't know what to ask for, nor did I have any supporting documentation. Now I did.

Happily, they contacted me first. Shortly after the first article on Eddie appeared, I got a call from Paul Petty, an examiner for the Board, suggesting that the family submit an application. Word had apparently come down from higher up. Petty sent us the application, which Buddha signed and returned on July 30.

THE WHITE HOUSE
WASHINGTON

July 27, 1999

Dear Mrs. Carter:

After reading the recent *U.S. News & World Report* feature article on your late husband, Sergeant Eddie Carter, I was saddened to learn of the additional injustice he had suffered by being denied reenlistment in the United States Army. Had I known this when I presented his Medal of Honor two years ago, I would have personally apologized to you and your family. On behalf of all Americans, I want to do so now.

Sergeant First Class Edward A. Carter, Jr., is an American hero. It was truly our loss that he was denied the opportunity to continue to serve in uniform the nation he so dearly loved.

Sincerely,

Bill Clinton

In a follow-up story on August 23, 1999, Joe Galloway reported my reaction: "The long-sought apology [from President Clinton] 'brings vindication and clears the false accusations which destroyed his military career and personal life,' says the soldier's daughter-in-law, Allene Carter. Her hope: that it will prompt the Army Board for

Correction of Military Records to correct all of his military records."

I knew that the Board for Correction had our application under consideration; hence my expression of hope that they would act favorably and promptly.

There were several things that we wanted done. In the first place, Joe Wilson had noticed that Sergeant Carter's rank on his headstone at Arlington was incorrect. It showed Eddie's rank as staff sergeant. In all of the excitement around the Medal of Honor ceremony and reinterment, I had not caught this error myself. But in fact, in 1949, Eddie had attained the rank of sergeant first class. We also knew that there were awards Eddie had won in the service that were not reflected in either his military records or on the headstone at Arlington, nor was his combat duty and combat military occupational specialty shown. Most important of all, of course, was clearing his name of any suggestion of disloyalty, with a new discharge certificate for his second enlistment for the period 1946–1949 that removed any statement of restrictions on his ability to reenlist. We also wanted the Adjutant General's Report corrected to record Eddie's service as an instructor to the California National Guard; this would require a separate action by the California Guard authorities.

Examiner Petty asked me for documentation to support the validity of these requests. This is where all my research and legwork paid off. I now had hundreds of pages of documents, letters, photographs, and other materials. I had organized it all into binders. I knew it all intimately, and I lived with it every day. To every query raised by Petty I was able to present copious documentation of what had transpired using the Army's own records, or correspondence sent by Army officials to others, such as the ACLU.

As it turned out, the Board for Correction met on August 26 to make a decision on our application. In September I received a copy of the report of the Board's proceedings and conclusions. The report made for the most satisfying reading that I had done in a long time. Several awards that Sergeant Carter had won during the war were not reflected on his discharge. This was corrected. The Board went further. Sergeant Carter was eligible for additional awards—a fact unknown to us—that were never granted, including the American Campaign Medal and Army of Occupation Medal. This was corrected. His discharge after World War II listed his race incorrectly as "white." This oddity was corrected.

Finally I came to the conclusion of the Board's proceeding: "The denial of reenlistment at the conclusion of the former service member's second enlistment was unjust. The allegations of interests by the former service member in conflict with those of the United States are determined to be unfounded based on a review of all evidence available. The denial of reenlistment should be rescinded with apologies."

It was such a bittersweet moment. I felt elated and emotionally exhausted at the same time.

I was pleased to get the Board's decision, but Buddha and I were clear in insisting that there must be a public apology. The falsity of the charges must be publicly stated, and Eddie's name cleared before the world. This idea was not warmly embraced, but the Army finally agreed to a public acknowledgment of what had happened.

On November 10, 1999, we found ourselves once again in Washington, D.C., at the Pentagon's Hall of Heroes. This time we were there for a ceremony at which an official apology was made by the Army for its banishment of Sergeant Edward Carter. Mildred was with us, although she didn't really understand what was happening. Eddie's sons Buddha and Redd sat with her as honored guests at the front of the room. Also present was Eddie's old commanding officer, Russell Blair. The room was filled with military and civilian guests, including Woodfred Jordan and Herbert Levy. Of course, our children Corey and Sandy and Redd's wife, Karen, were in the audience. Most of the major media sent reporters, and the ceremony was widely covered.

General John Keane, the Army's vice chief of staff, spoke for the Army. He told the story of Eddie's heroic action against the Germans at Speyer. Then he continued: "I recount Sergeant Carter's incredible story of bravery and determination because it reveals the depth of the

Vice Chief of Staff of the Army General John Keane presents duplicates of Sergeant Carter's medals to his sons, Edward III and William. (Courtesy U.S. Army)

injustice done to this great soldier after the war. We are here today to set the record straight," he said, "to acknowledge that a man of great personal courage, who served his country with honor and dignity, was denied the opportunity to reenlist, without explanation and without the opportunity to defend his good name and preserve his honor. Sergeant Carter . . . was an American hero who was denied the recognition he deserved and the opportunity to serve because of racial prejudice and the wave of

Former ACLU staff attorney Herbert Levy (center) with William and Edward III at the apology ceremony.

anticommunist hysteria that engulfed our nation after World War II.

"No words can right the wrong or undo the injustice that was done to Sergeant Carter. We must, however, acknowledge the mistake and apologize to his family and continue to honor the memory of this great soldier."

Later in the day we were transported to Arlington National Cemetery to lay a wreath and unveil the new headstone for Eddie's grave. It read:

Carter family members (left to right) William, Karen, Edward III, Allene,
Corey, Santalia, and Mildred at Sergeant Carter's grave
in Arlington National Cemetery, 1999.

EDWARD A. CARTER JR.

Medal of Honor

Sergeant First Class, U.S. Army

World War II

May 26, 1916–Jan. 30, 1963

Distinguished Service Cross, Bronze Star Medal

Purple Heart

Allene and Mildred view the corrected headstone at Sergeant Carter's grave.

Mildred's face lit up with recognition when she saw Eddie's name on the marker. She had a dignified, almost regal, presence.

There was one last step I needed to take. Following the ceremony of apology in Washington I went to Sacramento to the office of General Paul D. Munroe Jr., adjutant general of the California National Guard, to make my case for restoring Eddie's name to the history of the Guard. As General Munroe, an African American, reviewed the documentation I had brought with me, I thought how it would have pleased Eddie to know that a black man could now rise to a top position in the California National Guard. General Munroe said he took pride in knowing the history of the Sixth Engineer Combat Group, but he was unaware of the story of Sergeant Carter. He was very agreeable, he said, to correcting the official records and doing something to honor him.

General Munroe kept his word. On February 18, 2000, at a ceremony in Long Beach, he presented our family with a certificate correcting the National Guard's records. Subsequently, Sergeant Carter was honored by having the firing range at Camp Roberts at San Luis Obispo, where he trained the young black National Guardsmen, named for him. General Munroe also committed to having a new National Guard Armory being built in Azusa named for Sergeant Carter.

I had grown to love Eddie, and I felt great compassion for him. He was a hero, but he was first of all a man. I thought of the small boy growing up in Asia, hurt and angry, but who, as he matured into a man, transformed those feelings into a strong identification with other people who were victims of violence and injustice. He was a warrior, true, but he was a natural internationalist who always fought against injustice no matter where it might be found. I thought of the young man who forged his unhealed grief over the loss of his mother into passionate love for his wife, Mildred—a love that might have continued to flourish had they not been so battered by the Army, to which he was also wed. I thought of the hero, a man who fought courageously for a country he both loved and felt estranged from, who was then betrayed and banished because he refused to be cowed or intimidated. His vindication was long overdue.

OTHER SERGEANT CARTERS?

by Robert L. Allen

Although Tuesday, June 12, 2001, was a hot, muggy day in Norfolk, Virginia, for Allene Carter it was the finest day of the year. Allene was in Norfolk, along with members of her family and more than three hundred guests and media representatives, to take part in the christening of the M/V *SSG Edward A. Carter, Jr.,* an enormous military ammunition ship being named in honor of her deceased father-in-law. It was one of only a handful of military ships in U.S. history named for an African American. For Allene the occasion was a triumphant vindication after her years-long campaign to clear Sergeant Carter's name of unjust accusations used to hound him out of the Army. In this struggle Allene Carter also emerged as a hero, and she, too, was being honored on this historic day.

I first met Allene Carter in November 2000, when I was considering a proposal to collaborate with her on a book about Sergeant Carter's life. A tall, striking woman with a powerful presence, it soon became apparent that she was also possessed of enormous energy and a keen intelligence. We began to discuss the immense amount of research she had already undertaken and her hopes for the proposed book. Several thousand pages of documents, photographs, and news clippings were meticulously organized into three-ring binders, each carefully labeled and stored in chronological order. She had duplicate copies of some files organized into binders by subject areas. In addition, she had a small library of books and articles about World War II and the role of African Americans in the war. It is no exaggeration to say that in the quality and volume of her research, Allene Carter had accomplished the equivalent of what a Ph.D. graduate student would do in researching material for a dissertation—and she had done this with no formal training in academic research. I was impressed. Driven by a burning desire to learn the truth about Sergeant Carter, she had taught herself, with the help of mentors along the way, to do the necessary research work. Equally impressive, she had confronted the government with her findings and gained apologies—from President Clinton on down—for the military's unjust treatment of her father-in-law.

In a sense, Allene Carter had been preparing for most of her life for this great confrontation. The daughter of Jesse Vaughn, a staunch union organizer in the Chicago stockyards, she was raised to believe in fighting against injustice. Her father imbued her with a sense of the need for strong, militant unions. On her job she became a union steward in the Communications Workers of Amer-

Allene Carter proudly stands before the M/V SSG Edward A. Carter, Jr., *in Norfolk Shipyard, June 12, 2001. (Courtesy Norshipco)*

ica. With mentoring from union colleagues Bill Falcon, Bill Demers, and Michael Hartigan, she learned how to methodically fight and win grievance cases. One might say that her courageous campaign for justice for Sergeant Carter has been for her the ultimate grievance case.

Little did I suspect when we met in November and began working together that just over six months later we would be meeting again in Norfolk to celebrate the naming of a ship.

And it was a moving ceremony. Allene christened the

ship in the traditional way with a bottle of champagne, and then gave a short speech. The struggle to vindicate Sergeant Carter wasn't just about one family, she said. It was about changing our understanding of a generation. "When we go back to our respective communities," she told the audience, "we can take back a legacy with us. We can change history. We can reopen the history books to make corrections. I would ask that you hold on to what the Carter family has started, and continue on with us as we make a journey to ensure that the truth is recovered and preserved."

A warm round of applause greeted the Carters as they rose and stood proudly with Allene. Her face was radiant as the audience got to its feet and the applause continued in tribute to this remarkable African-American family.

Later in the day, as the festivities were ending, I joined a group of guests who were invited to tour the M/V *SSG Edward A. Carter, Jr.* Our guide told us that the ship was originally built in 1984 in Korea. At 950 feet in length it is longer than three football fields placed end to end. Under other names it operated as a container cargo vessel until it was brought to the Norfolk Shipbuilding & Drydock yard for conversion to an ammunition carrier for the U.S. Navy's Military Sealift Command. With a civilian crew of twenty and operated by Maersk Line, the ship will carry 2,500 containers in climate-controlled holds. As an ammunition carrier the mission of the M/V *Carter* will be to preposition ammunition supplies at sea for the U.S.

Army. In effect, the ship will serve as a floating ammunition depot available to supply U.S. military forces on short
notice, at sea or in a developed port. It will join thirty-five
other Military Sealift Command ships already deployed.
The ship was scheduled to set sail to a loading port in
North Carolina the morning after the naming ceremony.

As I toured the ship I couldn't help but recall the Port
Chicago explosion during World War II. My book *The
Port Chicago Mutiny* told the story of that disaster at a U.S.
Navy base in California. At the racially segregated base,
only black sailors were assigned to the dangerous work of
loading ammunition onto transport vessels under the
supervision of white officers. The black sailors had no
training in ammunition handling, and the white officers,
most of them untrained in the work, allowed unsafe working conditions. Because of racial discrimination, no black
sailor could become an officer or gain advancement
to other ratings. On July 17, 1944, a terrible explosion
occurred killing 320 men, two-thirds of whom were
African Americans, and wrecking the base. It was the
worst home front disaster of the war. In the aftermath,
when the surviving black sailors balked at returning to
handling ammunition, fifty were singled out, tried, and
unjustly convicted of mutiny. It was ironic, I thought, that
the Port Chicago book was about the explosion of an
ammunition ship and the mistreatment of black sailors in
World War II, and now I was working on a book about
the discrimination and mistreatment faced by an African-

American war hero who, half a century later, was being honored by having an ammunition ship named for him. No doubt the sailors who suffered at Port Chicago would be proud of Sergeant Carter and the vindication won for him by Allene Carter. The Port Chicago men would be pleased to see that the unionized workforce at the Norfolk shipyard was well trained and racially integrated, as was the crew of the ship.

But misfortune struck the M/V *Carter* within weeks. While the men were loading ammunition on July 14 at the Sunny Point Military Ocean Terminal in North Carolina, a fire broke out in the engine room. One man was killed in the fire and another drowned when he fell from the ship. Fortunately, the crew was able to confine the fire to the engine room and none of the ammunition exploded. An explosion aboard the M/V *Carter* would have made the Port Chicago explosion seem like a firecracker.

Over the following months the Carter was fully repaired, and as of March 2002, it was on station in the Diego Garcia area of the Indian Ocean.

The vindication of Sergeant Carter was a victory not just for the Carter family, but also for the African-American community and the nation. Allene Carter's quest showed that there is no statute of limitations on the struggle against injustice. Eddie Carter was not the only black soldier who was spied on, harassed, and mistreated by the military. During World War II many black soldiers were

unfairly targeted as suspicious and potential troublemak-
ers. In November 1999, Del Walters and the investigative
team of WJLA-TV, Channel 7 in Baltimore, produced a
two-part report on this mistreatment.

Walters and his reporters uncovered evidence that
"countless numbers of black soldiers who served in World
War II may have dirty little secrets hidden in their military files—accusations they were spies, rioters, even traitors, their mail intercepted, their conversations monitored,
their futures altered without reason." The investigation
concluded that "the Army routinely spied on black soldiers during World War II for a variety of reasons: espi-
onage, fears of rioting by black troops, even concerns
black soldiers would hoard ammunition. In most cases, as
was the case with Sergeant Carter, the charges were
unfounded, but the damage had already been done." Soldiers were not the only targets. Black reporters, such as
the respected journalist Alfred Duckett, who wrote for
Ebony magazine and the Baltimore *Afro-American* newspaper, were also targeted as alleged traitors. Calls for a congressional hearing were made in the televised report.
"How many other Sergeant Carters remain out there?"
Walters asked.

"My hope," Allene told me, "is that Sergeant Carter's
story will encourage other veterans and their families to
press on in their quest for justice. An apology should be
made and restitution offered to the families of all veterans
whose military records and good names were stained by
unjust accusations."

ARCHIVES

Documents pertaining to the performance and treatment of black soldiers in World War II, as well as military intelligence and FBI surveillance of black soldiers and civilians are located at the National Archives, College Park, Maryland.

Important archives of the Abraham Lincoln Brigade are located at the Library of Brandeis University, Waltham, Massachusetts.

Historical documentation of California National Guard units may be found in the California State Library located in Sacramento.

The archives of the American Civil Liberties Union are located at the Seeley Mudd Library of Princeton University in Princeton, New Jersey.

Files of the *Pentecost* and the *Standard Bearer* newspapers may be found at the Wesleyan Archives and Historical Library in Indianapolis, Indiana.

Papers of President Harry Truman are located in the Harry S. Truman Library, Independence, Missouri.

SELECTED BIBLIOGRAPHY

Baker, Vernon J., with Ken Olsen. *Lasting Valor*. Columbus, Miss.: Genesis Press, 1997.

Barboza, Steven, ed. *The African American Book of Values*. New York: Doubleday, 1998.

Blumenson, Martin. *Mark Clark: The Last of the Great World War II Commanders*. New York: Congdon & Weed, 1984.

Bradstreet, Ken. *The Hellcats* (2 vols.). Paducah, Ky.: Turner Publishing, 1987.

Breuer, William B. *Storming Hitler's Rhine: The Allied Assault, February–March 1945*. New York: St. Martin's Press, 1985.

Clark, Mark W. *From the Danube to the Yalu*. New York: Harper & Brothers, 1954.

———. *Calculated Risk*. New York: Harper & Brothers, 1950.

Collum, Danny, ed. *African Americans in the Spanish Civil War*. New York: G. K. Hall, 1992.

Converse Elliott V., III, Daniel K. Gibran, et al. *The Exclusion of Black Soldiers from the Medal of Honor in World War II*. Jefferson, N.C.: McFarland, 1997.

Edgerton, Robert B. *Heroism: Black Soldiers in America's Wars*. Boulder, Colo.: Westview, 2001.

Eisenhower, John S. D. *The Bitter Woods: The Battle of the Bulge*. New York: Da Capo Press, 1969.

Ellis, John. *Cassino: The Hollow Victory.* New York: McGraw-Hill, 1984.

Forty, George. *Patton's Third Army at War.* London: Arms and Armour Press, 1976.

Jensen, Joan. *Army Surveillance in America, 1775–1980.* New Haven: Yale University Press, 1991.

Lee, Ulysses. *The Employment of Negro Troops.* Washington, D.C.: Center of Military History U.S. Army, 1963.

Nalty, Bernard C. *Strength for the Fight: A History of Black Americans in the Military.* New York: The Free Press, 1986.

Payne, Robert. *Chiang Kai-shek.* New York: Weybright & Talley, 1969.

Province, Charles M. *Patton's Third Army.* New York: Hippocrene, 1992.

Seagrave, Sterling. *The Soong Dynasty.* New York: Harper & Row, 1985.

Tuchman, Barbara W. *Stilwell and the American Experience in China 1911–45.* New York: Macmillan, 1970.

Weigley, Russell F. *Eisenhower's Lieutenants: The Campaigns of France and Germany, 1944–1945.* Bloomington: Indiana University Press, 1981.

White, Theodore H., and Annalee Jacoby. *Thunder out of China.* New York: Da Capo Press, 1974.

Wilson, Joe, Jr. *The 761st "Black Panther" Tank Battalion in World War II.* Jefferson, N.C.: McFarland, 1999.

Yates, James. *Mississippi to Madrid.* Seattle: Open Hand, 1989.